IMPROVE
— YOUR —
WORD
POWER

Test and Build
Your Vocabulary

IMPROVE
—YOUR—
WORD
POWER

Test and Build
Your Vocabulary

CAROLINE TAGGART

Michael O'Mara Books Limited

First published in Great Britain in 2019 by
Michael O'Mara Books Limited
9 Lion Yard
Tremadoc Road
London SW4 7NQ

A CIP catalogue record for this book is available from the British Library.

Papers used by Michael O'Mara Books Limited are natural, recyclable products
made from wood grown in sustainable forests. The manufacturing processes
conform to the environmental regulations of the country of origin.

ISBN: 978-1-78929-116-2 in hardback print format
ISBN: 978-1-78929-183-4 in ebook format

1 2 3 4 5 6 7 8 9 10

Cover design by Ana Bjezancevic
Designed and typeset by Ed Pickford

Printed and bound by CPI Group (UK) Ltd, Croydon, CR0 4YY

Follow us on Twitter @OMaraBooks
www.mombooks.com

Contents

Introduction

It's one of life's great unsung pleasures to be able to use the right word in the right place at the right time. OK, it may not compare with the right amount of chocolate in the right place at the right time, or a warm fire and the right old movie on TV, but it's up there.

A good vocabulary is more than a pleasure, though. It's a tool. Using words accurately enables you to make a distinction between two similar things, to make a difference between *sensual* and *sensuous* or *fortuitous* and *fortunate*. Use the right word and you'll never have to say, 'Oh, you know what I mean', because you will have *said* what you mean. If this seems pedantic, consider this thought from the late wordsmith Fritz Spiegl: 'You *can* use a chisel as a screwdriver, but it won't do the job as well, and it will never be quite as good a chisel again.'

With this in mind, this book sets out, in thirty-five themed quizzes, to test your word power and, with any luck, occasionally improve it. Alphabetically, it ranges from *abject* to *zeitgeist*; it includes quizzes on words from French and words from Asian languages; on words to do with cinema, philosophy and money. There are quizzes on words about joy and sorrow, compliments and insults. And, just for fun, the book ends with two sections on words that are simply a joy to use. Scattered through it are boxes on random subjects such as words that are easily confused and the disappointing fact that *gnomic* and *pixels* are nothing to do with *gnomes* and *pixies*.

There's no formal scoring system, so let's just suggest that a score of 15 (out of 20 in each case) is not bad, while a score of under 10 is not great. It's up to you how competitive you make it, with friends and family or with yourself. The important thing is to enjoy yourself. If you learn something along the way, so much the better.

Animal, vegetable or mineral

What better way to start a quiz book than with a reference to another quiz? All the words here could fit under one of the headings 'animal', 'vegetable' or 'mineral' – but do you know what they mean?

Antimony a) A medicinal herb b) A small mammal c) A silvery metal

Borage a) A bird b) A herb c) A tree

Calabrese a) A breed of horse b) A build-up of salts in the body c) A sort of broccoli

Dotterel a) Another name for the aardvark b) A metallic element c) A shore bird

Eland a) A breed of duck b) A large antelope c) A section of an electrical circuit

Frigate a) A beetle b) A mushroom c) A seabird

Gallium a) A mushroom b) The scientific name for a chicken c) A silvery element

Jacaranda a) An African antelope b) An ornamental tree c) A South American bird

Kohlrabi a) An alkaline metal b) A form of cabbage c) A species of albatross

Leatherjacket a) A fibrous mineral b) The larva of certain insects c) Another name for the sweet potato

Moa a) An extinct New Zealand bird b) A South African fruit c) A South American monkey

Ngaio a) A bird b) A mineral c) A tree

Ormolu a) A decorative metal alloy b) A form of cabbage c) A songbird

Poinsettia a) A flowering plant b) A North American snake c) A type of rabbit

Quagga a) An extinct horse b) A moss c) A seabird

Ratel a) A fierce animal b) A metal c) A small tree used in hedges

Tungsten a) A greyish element b) A parrot c) A relative of the rhinoceros

Vermiculite a) A mineral used in gardening b) A mushroom c) A type of worm

Yggdrasil a) A mushroom b) A mythological tree c) A type of fern

Zircon a) An extinct horse b) A mineral used as a gemstone c) Another name for the zebra finch

Answers

Antimony c) A silvery metal, used in semiconductors.

Borage b) A herb with blue, star-shaped flowers. Very pretty when frozen in ice cubes and added to drinks. (Pretty in the garden, too.)

Calabrese c) A sort of broccoli, that Dayglo-green sprouting kind that looks like something from outer space.

Dotterel c) A shore bird, a type of plover.

Eland b) A large antelope, the largest in Africa, with impressive spiralling horns.

Frigate c) A seabird, known for its broad wingspan and habit of stealing food from the beaks of other birds in flight.

Gallium c) A silvery element whose most useful characteristic is that it is liquid at a wide range of temperatures. The scientific name for a chicken is *Gallus gallus*.

Jacaranda b) An ornamental tree with conspicuous blue-purple flowers.

Kohlrabi b) A form of cabbage with an edible root or bulb that looks a bit like a turnip. Pronounced *coal-rah-bee*.

Leatherjacket b) The larva of certain insects, particularly the crane fly or daddy-longlegs.

Moa a) An extinct New Zealand bird, resembling an enormous emu.

Ngaio c) A small tree or shrub, also from New Zealand, with relations across Australia and the South Pacific. Pronounced *nigh–o*.

Ormolu a) A decorative metal alloy, usually gold in colour and often used to embellish furniture and clocks.

Poinsettia a) A flowering plant with red foliage, popular at Christmas.

Quagga a) An extinct horse- or zebra-like animal with stripes only on the front of its body.

Ratel a) A fierce animal, related to the weasels and also known as the honey badger. No more than 28 cm (11 in) high and weighing 10–15 kilograms (22–33 lb), it can still have a go at a lion. Think wolverine with attitude.

Tungsten a) A greyish element with a variety of industrial uses. Its name means 'heavy stone' in Swedish.

Vermiculite a) A mineral used in gardening, as a sort of potting compost for young plants. A different form can also be used in sound-proofing and fire resistance. Vermiculite splits into thin flakes when heated, a characteristic that made someone think of worms or the tracks they leave – hence the name, which comes (like the fine pasta known as *vermicelli*) from the Latin for worm.

Yggdrasil b) A mythological tree from Norse tradition: usually said to be an ash, it is the centre of the cosmos, binding various worlds together.

Zircon b) A mineral used as a gemstone, occurring in various colours from red to green, as well as in a colourless form.

CONFUSABLES

adverse/averse

Adverse means unfavourable, hostile, as in *adverse weather conditions* or *adverse criticism*; *averse* is unwilling or disinclined and is often used in the negative: *I'm not averse to going with you, as long as you don't expect me to drive.*

Some colourful phrases

We seem to love endowing colours with different qualities – green is eco-friendly or naïve, blue is sad or pornographic, gold and silver are privileged. Do you know the meaning of these colourful expressions?

Blackball a) To cheat at roulette b) To vote against someone c) To win at bowls

Black sheep a) Someone who mindlessly follows the example of others b) Someone who is considered a disgrace to the family c) A union member who goes to work while others are on strike

Blue-blooded a) Aristocratic b) Cowardly c) Hot-tempered

Blue collar a) Aristocratic b) Involved in manual labour c) Possessive, jealous

In a brown study a) Deep in thought b) Depressed c) Sycophantic

Golden handshake A generous payment made … a) in recognition of a job well done b) when you narrowly fail to win a jackpot or star prize c) when you retire or leave your job

Green card A card permitting you to … a) live and work in the United States b) park without payment c) return to the sports field after time in the 'sin bin'

(To have) green fingers a) To be envious, especially of other people's money b) To have a natural talent for gardening c) To be unsophisticated, foolishly trusting

Grey area One that is a) dull b) not clearly defined c) set aside for future building development

In the pink a) Healthy and happy b) In uncertain financial circumstances c) Young and sexually attractive

Purple prose Writing that is … a) evocative of winter b) unnecessarily elaborate c) very dull

Caught red-handed a) Caught and bowled (in cricket) or by the pitcher (in baseball) b) Caught in the act c) Caught napping

Red herring a) A distraction b) A fish dish popular in India c) An untrustworthy person

Red-letter day a) A day when disaster strikes b) An important occasion c) The last working day of the month

Red tape a) Luxurious extras included in the price of a holiday b) Tape scattered in celebration during a procession c) Time-consuming official procedure

(To view the world through) rose-tinted spectacles a) To be irritatingly cheerful b) To be unnecessarily pessimistic c) To be unrealistically optimistic

(To be born with a) silver spoon (in your mouth) a) To have a knack of getting out of trouble b) To inherit wealth and good fortune b) To speak fluently but rather glibly

White-knuckle a) Always ready to start a fight b) Cowardly c) Frightening

Yellow-bellied a) Cowardly b) Disloyal c) A habitual liar

Answers

Blackball b) To vote against someone. In the eighteenth century, members of a club would hold a secret ballot to decide whether or not to admit a new applicant. Putting a white ball into the urn said yes, a black ball said no. Nowadays, the expression has a broader meaning – to ostracize or turn a cold shoulder to someone.

Black sheep b) Someone who is considered a disgrace to the family. This isn't a racist comment so much as a financial one – a black sheep's wool couldn't be dyed, so it was worth less than that of the rest of the (white) flock.

Blue-blooded a) Aristocratic. This *is* a racist comment, deriving from the Moorish invasion of Spain in the eighth century. The Spaniards considered themselves socially superior to the Moors, so were proud of the veins showing blue under their paler skins.

Blue collar b) Involved in manual labour, and therefore likely to wear a blue overall, as opposed to a *white-collar* office worker, who traditionally wore a white shirt and a tie. An expression coined when all workers, at whatever level, were assumed to be male.

In a brown study a) Deep in thought. The colour brown used to be associated with sadness, so a brown study was originally a gloomy one; now it just tends to mean 'Oh, sorry, I was miles away.'

Golden handshake c) A generous payment made when you retire or leave your job. Any idiom to do with gold involves money, good fortune or both. A golden handshake tends to be given to people who might be considered to have quite enough money already, such as executives who have been involved in a scandal and forced to resign, but still have to be paid off. Generously.

Green card a) A card permitting you to live and work in the United States. This is a literal description: when you are given this permission, you are issued with a card, which happens to be green. Or greenish.

(To have) green fingers b) To have a natural talent for gardening, because green is the colour of horticulture and growth. Sometimes 'a green thumb'.

Grey area b) Not clearly defined, not set down in black and white. A grey area is one about which it is hard to make up your mind, because you can see arguments for both sides.

In the pink a) Healthy and happy. 'The pink' is the peak of condition, the height of fashion, any desirable state.

Purple prose b) Writing that is unnecessarily elaborate. Purple is the colour of richness – being born *in the purple* means being royal, or something close to it. With *purple prose* (or *a purple patch* or *passage*) this richness goes over the top and becomes excessively ornate.

Caught red-handed b) Caught in the act. Originally you would have been poaching, with red hands from the blood of the stag you shouldn't have killed; now you can be caught red-handed in the course of any crime or misdemeanour.

Red herring a) A distraction. A red (smoked) herring has a particularly strong smell; if you draw it across the fox's trail during a hunting expedition, it distracts the hounds. Nowadays, a red herring is more usually found in a detective story: it's a piece of irrelevant information planted by the author to distract the reader from following the genuine clues.

Red-letter day b) An important occasion, originally a saint's day or other holiday, traditionally printed in red on a calendar.

Red tape c) Time-consuming official procedure, so called because official documents, which had to be dealt with before anything useful could be done, were tied up with red tape. The tape scattered during a procession is *ticker tape*.

(To view the world through) rose-tinted spectacles c) To be unrealistically optimistic, seeing the good side of everything. This could, of course, involve being irritatingly cheerful, but mindless optimism is the defining factor.

(To be born with a) silver spoon (in your mouth) b) To inherit wealth and good fortune. Not necessarily as lucrative as a golden handshake (see above), but still an advantage.

White-knuckle c) Frightening, usually in the expression *a white-knuckle ride*. This originated in the idea of a ride at a funfair that was designed to be scary and made you grip the safety rail so tightly that your knuckles went white. It can now be used metaphorically, too: giving a series of high-pressure presentations at work might be described as *a white-knuckle ride*. There's the sense of a happy outcome, though: just as you usually emerge unscathed from a frightening experience at a funfair, so you normally come through those *white-knuckle* presentations having won the contract.

Yellow-bellied a) Cowardly. It's not clear why yellow came to be associated with cowardice – there are many creatures, from woodpeckers to whales and including rattlesnakes, that boast a yellow-bellied species, but none has been pinpointed as of a particularly nervous disposition. The expression became popular in the American Wild West in the nineteenth century, so it may refer (insultingly) to the supposedly sallow skin of the Mexicans with whom the US was at war, but no one is really sure.

Words about family and friends

It's easy enough to talk about uncles and aunts and cousins, but sometimes we want something more specific or more grandiose, and sometimes those relationships take on extra, subtler meanings ... See how you get on with these.

Atavistic a) Having primitive characteristics b) Overwhelmingly protective c) Pertaining to a grandparent

Avuncular Pertaining to or like ... a) a cousin b) a grandparent c) an uncle

Cadet a) A nephew b) A second cousin or cousin 'once removed' c) A younger son or brother

Camaraderie a) An incestuous relationship b) Betrothal c) Friendship

Confidant a) A close friend b) A lover c) A sister or brother

Connubial Pertaining to ... a) cousins b) marriage c) trusted friends

Dowager a) A minor beneficiary of a will b) An unmarried aunt c) A widow

Filial Pertaining to ... a) betrothal b) the family home c) a son or daughter

Fraternize a) To associate on friendly terms b) To become engaged c) To include someone in your will

Matriarchy A society dominated by … a) brothers b) married couples c) women

Mentor a) The best man at a wedding b) A trusted adviser c) An uncle

Morganatic Pertaining to … a) an acrimonious divorce b) a marriage between two people of unequal rank c) a wedding present

Nepotism a) Favouritism b) Incest c) An unexpected inheritance

Paternalistic a) Affectionate b) Overly protective and fussy c) Stern and forbidding

Patrimony a) Fatherly affection b) An inheritance from your father c) Same-sex marriage

Primogeniture a) Being conceived but not born before your parents are married b) The earliest known ancestor on a family tree c) The system whereby the eldest son automatically inherits his family's titles and estates

Progeny a) Descendants, offspring b) Inheritance c) Legitimacy

Scion a) Any descendant or young member of a family b) A sister c) A younger son or daughter

Sodality a) Companionship b) A formal betrothal c) A group of women

Sorority a) Being alienated from your family b) Companionship c) A group of women

Answers

Atavistic a) Having primitive characteristics, reverting to an earlier type whose characteristics have skipped a generation or more. From a Latin word meaning great-great-great-grandfather.

Avuncular c) Pertaining to or resembling an uncle – friendly, helpful and protective towards a younger person. The equivalent word for an aunt is *materteral*, which the *OED* describes as 'humorous, rare'; it's not a word you'd expect to use without having to explain it, and strictly speaking it applies only to a mother's sister, not a father's. Latin was particular about that sort of thing.

Cadet c) A younger son or brother, hence the *cadet branch* of a family, which was descended from a younger son. The concept of a military or naval *cadet* arose because many younger sons traditionally forged careers in the armed forces while their eldest brother stayed at home, learning to manage their father's estate, which he would eventually inherit (see *patrimony* and *primogeniture*, below).

Camaraderie c) Friendship, matiness, the trust and familiarity that exist between friends or comrades. From the French *camarade*, a comrade or pal.

Confidant a) A close (male) friend, one in whom you confide. The female equivalent is *confidante*. Not to be confused with *confident*, which is an adjective meaning certain, sure of yourself.

Connubial b) Pertaining to marriage. Often used humorously and with a sly reference to sex, particularly in the expression *connubial bliss*.

Dowager c) A widow who retains property or a title belonging to her late husband. Often used in conjunction with the title – a *dowager duchess* or *dowager countess*.

Filial c) Pertaining to a son or daughter: *filial respect* and *filial affection* are emotions that – in an ideal world – you feel towards your parents.

Fraternize a) To associate on friendly terms, from the Latin for brother. It sounds harmless enough, but *fraternizing with the enemy* in time of war could get you shot.

Matriarchy c) A society dominated by women, from *mater*, the Latin for mother. You often hear this word on wildlife programmes, where elephant herds in particular are dominated by a powerful female known as the *matriarch*.

Mentor b) A trusted adviser, a tutor or guide who takes a younger student under his or her wing. The original Mentor appears in Homer's *Odyssey*: he is tutor to Odysseus's son Telemachus while Odysseus is away at the Trojan War.

Morganatic b) Pertaining to a marriage between two people of unequal rank. In such a marriage, the lower-ranking person is not raised to the higher rank and their children don't inherit the titles and property. Not desperately important unless you're an aristocrat.

Nepotism a) Favouritism, generally in the workplace, giving jobs or promotion to relatives or (more loosely) friends. From the Latin *nepos*, which meant both a nephew and a grandson.

Paternalistic b) Overly protective and fussy. From the Latin *pater*, meaning father, but showing the negative qualities of a father. Often used of a government that makes too many decisions on behalf of its people and denies individual liberty – the sort of government that is also, in an odd shift of gender, known as a *nanny state*.

Patrimony b) An inheritance from your father. Again from the Latin *pater*. The *-mony* part has nothing to do with *money* but comes from Latin via French as a common ending for abstract nouns (*ceremony*, *matrimony*, *testimony* and so on).

Primogeniture c) The system whereby the eldest son automatically inherits his family's titles and estates, to the exclusion of any sisters or younger brothers. From the Latin for first-born, though it definitely meant first-born male.

Progeny a) Descendants, offspring, especially when there are a lot of them: *the photo showed my grandfather surrounded by his numerous* *progeny.* A word of complicated origins, though the *-geny* (like the *gen* in *primogeniture*, above) is related to all sorts of other words to do with having children, including *genital, generation* and, oddly enough, *genius.*

Scion a) Any descendant or young member of a family. From an Old French word meaning the shoot or tip of a plant, also found in gardening-speak to denote part of a plant (such as an apple tree) used to form a graft.

Sodality a) Companionship, fellowship, particularly in the Catholic Church, where the word means a charitable society or one formed for mutual support. From the Latin *sodalis,* a comrade.

Sorority c) A group of women, usually a women's society at an American university, the female equivalent of a *fraternity.* From the Latin *soror,* meaning a sister.

Did you know?

Gnomic – referring to a short but perhaps rather obscure statement – has nothing to do with gnomes. It derives from the Greek for *to know.* The word *gnome* to denote a race of diminutive spirits said to guard the Earth's treasures was coined arbitrarily by the sixteenth-century Swiss physician Paracelsus, who made a habit of inventing words when it suited him.

Sadly, *pixels* – the tiny areas on a computer screen from which images are composed – are nothing to do with pixies, either. They come from *pix* or *pics,* the diminutive of pictures.

Words about thoughts and ideas

Some of these fall under the heading 'philosophy'; others are just words about different aspects of thinking, and a few suggest thinking about something difficult or obscure.

Arcane a) Illogical b) Mysterious c) Unresolved

Ascetic a) Indifferent b) Practising self-denial c) Studying beauty and taste

Cogent a) Convincing b) Lucky c) Thoughtful

Determinism The theory that ... a) happiness can be achieved only through hard work b) the end justifies the means c) there is no such thing as freedom of choice

Dichotomy a) Division b) Oppression c) Rule by two people or bodies

Elucidate a) To clarify b) To grant the vote c) To pardon

Empirical a) Based on direct observation b) Imperialistic, conquering c) Liberating

Hedonism A doctrine that advocates ... a) the importance of education b) the pursuit of pleasure c) the supremacy of the male sex

Heuristic a) Dictatorial b) Guiding c) Pleasure-seeking

Hypothetical a) False b) Over-particular, nit-picking
c) Suggested but not proven

Machiavellian a) Cunning and opportunistic b) Determined by
arithmetical calculation c) Tightly controlled

Nihilism A philosophy that … a) denies the existence of God
b) promotes moderation in all things c) rejects all values

Pantheism A philosophy that … a) makes sacrifices to animal
deities b) promotes physical fitness as an ideal c) sees God in
everything

Phenomenology A philosophy based on the study of … a) great
pleasures b) personal experience c) UFOs

Pragmatism Making a decision based on … a) the likelihood
of financial gain b) practical considerations rather than theory
c) previous experience

Proselytize a) To convert someone from one belief to another
b) To debate c) To preach at tedious length

Putative a) Argumentative b) Disrespectful c) Likely

Ruminate a) To change sides in a debate or argument b) To express
strong views c) To ponder

Socratic a) Excluding women from political debate b) Seeking
answers through questioning c) Studying social behaviour

Stoical a) Indulging in faulty reasoning b) Resigned
c) Self-indulgent

Answers

Arcane b) Mysterious, requiring secret knowledge in order to be understood: *the guide's arcane pieces of information brought Ancient Egypt to life – we learned more about the burial rituals of the Pharaohs than we could possibly need to know.*

Ascetic b) Practising self-denial, giving up worldly comforts, especially for religious reasons. From a Greek word meaning exercise, it originally referred to the sort of abstinence practised by athletes in training; in the early Christian Church, it meant monks who ate sparingly, slept on hard wooden beds and got up in the middle of the night to say prayers. Many other religions include an element of *asceticism*: Muslims fasting during Ramadan is one example. The philosophy concerned with beauty and taste is *aesthetics*, while indifferent could be *apathetic*.

Cogent a) Convincing, persuasive, difficult to argue against, as in *cogent reasoning*.

Determinism c) The theory that there is no such thing as freedom of choice, that any human action is pre-determined by past events or the current set of circumstances. The idea that the end justifies the means is generally thought of as *Machiavellian* (see below).

Dichotomy a) Division into two parts, usually sharply distinguished and mutually exclusive: *the dichotomy between rich and poor* or *between pacifism and warmongering*. Rule by two people or bodies is a *diarchy*, as opposed to a *monarchy*, which has only one person is charge (for other *mon-* words, see *One or many?*, page 104).

Elucidate a) To clarify, make *lucid*: *I could see they were baffled by what I had said, so I tried to elucidate by cutting down on the technical terms.*

Empirical a) Based on direct observation, experiment or experience as opposed to reasoning or theory: *empirical evidence suggests that the new drug will protect against heart disease, but there hasn't yet been a proper study.*

Hedonism b) A doctrine that advocates the pursuit of pleasure; strictly speaking a school of philosophy in Ancient Greece that also advised keeping pain and adversity under control. In modern use, it may mean nothing more philosophical than lolling around in your pyjamas and binge-watching the latest political thriller.

Heuristic b) Guiding, specifically a method of teaching that encourages students to find things out for themselves. A *heuristic computer program* solves problems by (very rapid) trial and error, rather than by following a strict algorithm. From the Greek for 'to find' and related to *eureka* (literally 'I have found it').

Hypothetical c) Suggested but not proven. A *hypothesis* is a 'best guess': you can work on the basis that it is true until someone comes up with something better, or until you've carried out enough experiments to prove or disprove it. *Hypothetical* is most frequently used in the phrase *a hypothetical question*, which may be asked of an expert witness in court, seeking a general opinion rather than one specific to the case; or in a less formal context, referring to a set of circumstances that is unlikely to arise: *to ask a hypothetical question, do you think I look better in diamonds or emeralds?*

Machiavellian a) Cunning and opportunistic, in the manner of the Italian Renaissance politician Niccolò Machiavelli. He wrote a book called *The Prince*, full of *pragmatic* (see below) advice on how someone in power should maintain his position: perhaps his most famous maxim was that it was safer to be feared than to be loved.

Nihilism c) A philosophy that rejects all values, religions and laws, either from a sense of despair and a belief that life has no meaning, or as a form of terrorism (particularly in Russia in the early twentieth century) intended to overthrow the establishment. From the Latin *nihil*, meaning nothing, which also gives us *annihilate*, to destroy absolutely, to reduce to nothing.

Pantheism c) A philosophy that sees God in everything – humanity, the natural world, the universe, you name it. From the Greek for all (*pan-*) and god (*theos*), which also give us, on the one hand, *panacea* (a cure-all), *pandemic* (a widespread epidemic) and Douglas Adams' *Pan Galactic Gargle Blaster* (a cocktail presumably available throughout the galaxy);

and, on the other, *atheism* (rejection of belief in God), *monotheism* (belief in one god) and *theology* (the study of God). See also *apotheosis*, page 185.

Phenomenology b) Describing personal experience. A philosophy focusing on the detailed study of what actually happened, rather than trying to draw conclusions about its meaning.

Pragmatism b) Making a decision based on practical considerations rather than theory: a *pragmatic approach to social reform* would take into account what was affordable, practicable and likely to lose fewest votes rather than aiming for the ideal.

Proselytize a) To convert someone from one belief to another, thus making a *proselyte* of them. There's the sense in *proselytize* that you have put strenuous effort into the conversion; and in *proselyte* that the convert is likely to be more enthusiastic about the new set-up than someone who was born and raised in it. Pronounced *pross-i-light-eyes*, it's nothing to do with *prose*, but comes from the Greek for a new arrival.

Putative c) Likely, widely regarded as: *when my son showed no interest in the business, my niece became my putative successor*. From the Latin for to think or consider.

Ruminate c) To ponder, to chew over slowly, in the manner of a cow chewing the cud. The comparison isn't a random one: the word comes from the same Latin source as *rumen*, the first compartment of the stomach of a *ruminant*, an animal that chews the cud.

Socratic b) Seeking answers through questioning, like the Ancient Greek philosopher Socrates. His approach to truth-seeking was to affect to know nothing, but by persistent questioning to show up the flaws in another person's arguments or opinions.

Stoical b) Resigned, prepared to put up with whatever life throws at you. From the Stoic philosophers of Ancient Greece, so called because they met under a *stoa* or porch.

A change is as good as a rest

All the words in this list begin with a prefix meaning the same or different, changing or being together. That isn't always obvious from the meaning of the whole word, but see how you get on.

Alienation a) Colonization (of an area) by a non-native plant or creature b) Feeling isolated c) Slander

Allotrope a) One of the forms in which an element can exist b) A rhetorical question c) A share or portion

Altercation a) A change in the weather b) A drug prescribed to treat specific symptoms c) A heated argument

Heterodoxy a) Going against established beliefs b) Having many colours c) An order of insects

Homeopathy A way of treating disease that ... a) allows it to take its course b) induces fever c) uses what causes the symptoms as a 'medicine'

Homeostasis a) Arranging items of a similar size or appearance together b) Maintaining equilibrium c) Rhyming

Homogeneous a) Having the same ancestors b) Maintaining a steady temperature c) Uniform

Homophone A word that ... a) begins with the same sound as others that occur in quick succession b) is pronounced like another, but spelled differently c) means the same as another

Metacarpus a) Bones in the hand b) A chemical process
c) An outer galaxy

Metadata a) Data about data b) Information that changes with the
passage of time c) A literal translation

Metamorphosis a) Change of form or substance b) Sterility
c) Weather conditions

Metaphor a) A body of data b) A figure of speech c) A substance
capable of emitting light

Metaphysical Concerned with ... a) gender issues b) the nature of
reality c) the study of rocks

Symbiosis a) Balance b) Mutual dependency c) Vulnerability, a
tendency to fall ill

Symposium a) A conference b) A friendly relationship c) A short
musical piece

Synaesthesia a) Administering drugs b) A rock formation
c) A sensation experienced by a sense other than the one stimulated

Synapse a) A figure of speech b) Mumbling or mispronunciation
c) Part of the nervous system

Syncopation a) A drinking bout b) Ensuring several things
happen at the same time c) The 'offbeat' rhythm used in jazz

Synergy a) An ecclesiastical council b) The symptoms of a
particular disease c) Working together

Synthetic a) Artificial b) Elastic, stretchy c) Related to grammatical
structure

Answers

Alienation b) Feeling isolated from society. Not the same as loneliness; more not belonging. From a Latin word for other that also gives us *alien*.

Allotrope a) One of the forms in which an element can exist: diamond, coal and graphite are all *allotropes* of carbon. *Allo-* comes from the Greek for different and *trope* from the Greek for style.

Altercation c) A heated argument: *there were sounds of an altercation from next door – shouting, banging doors and smashing crockery.* From another Latin word for other, which also gives us *alter*, *alternate* and *alternative*.

Heterodoxy a) Going against established beliefs, as opposed to *orthodoxy*, which is going *with* established beliefs. Anything beginning with *hetero-* is likely to mean other or different (*heterosexual*, being attracted to the opposite sex, is the only common word, but there are lots of technical ones to do with having different forms, different colours or a different arrangement of toes).

Homeopathy c) A way of treating disease that uses what causes the symptoms as a 'medicine'. The idea is that a tiny dose of a substance that in a healthy person would, for example, induce fever will relieve the fever in a sufferer.

Homeostasis b) Maintaining equilibrium, usually within an animal's metabolism, as when the immune system leaps into action against bacteria or a virus.

Homogeneous c) Uniform, composed of similar or identical elements. It is also spelled *homogenous* and is related to *homogenization*, the process of breaking up the fat content in milk so that it is distributed evenly throughout, rather than sitting in a creamy layer on the top. The prefix *homo-* comes from the Greek for same and has nothing to do with the Latin for man, which crops up in expressions such as *Homo sapiens*.

Homophone b) A word that is pronounced like another, but spelled differently. English is full of these – *bear* and *bare*, *feat* and *feet*, *wait* and *weight*, and so on. A word that begins with the same sound as others that occur in quick succession is *alliteration*, while a word that means the same as another is a *synonym*.

Metacarpus a) Bones in the hand. *Meta-* often means 'change', but can also mean 'after' or 'beyond'. The *metacarpus* – the five long bones that form the skeleton of the human hand, and their equivalent in other animals – is therefore *beyond* the *carpus* or wrist. These bones are often referred to as the *metacarpals*; in the foot, the *tarsus* is the ankle and the *metatarsus* or *metatarsal bones* are the skeleton of the foot itself.

Metadata a) Data about data. The *metadata* about a scholarly article, for example, might include its title, abstract, author, date of publication, the journal in which it appeared and much more – but not its full content.

Metamorphosis a) Change of form or substance. Franz Kafka's novella *Metamorphosis* gives a clear idea of the concept: *When Gregor Samsa woke up one morning from unsettling dreams, he found himself changed in his bed into a monstrous vermin.* Less alarmingly, caterpillars *metamorphose* into butterflies or moths and ugly ducklings into swans.

Metaphor b) A figure of speech – a comparison that says something *is* something: *He may seem stern, but really he's a pussycat – I can always get what I want from him.* The other figure of speech commonly used in comparisons is a *simile*, which would have said that this stern man was *like* a pussycat.

Metaphysical b) Concerned with the nature of reality, going *beyond* physics to find out what we can know about our own existence, about God and so forth. This isn't really what the Metaphysical Poets of the seventeenth century did: they wrote with intense feeling, but used a lot of elaborate imagery – *metaphysical* was an insulting description later thrown at them by Samuel Johnson, who couldn't stand them.

Symbiosis b) Mutual dependency, as when two species of plant or animal live closely together. It's often used to describe a relationship in which both parties benefit, such as when an insect feeding on a plant's pollen spreads that pollen and fertilizes other plants. Scientists call this *mutualism.* Symbiosis can also refer to a set-up in which one participant benefits and the other is not actually harmed – if a spider weaves a web between branches of a tree, the tree neither wins nor loses. If you want to impress, you can call this *commensalism.* But in both cases, *symbiosis* will do. Words beginning *sym-* or *syn-* are likely to mean something to do with 'with' or 'together' – *symbiosis* is literally living together.

Symposium a) A conference, originally (in Ancient Greece) a gathering for the purpose of drinking and enjoying intellectual conversation. Nowadays, likely to be an academic gathering at which papers on a specific topic are presented and the drinking happens afterwards.

Synaesthesia c) A sensation experienced by a sense other than the one stimulated, as when you react to a smell or a sound by imagining or actually seeing a colour. Not everyone experiences this: about one person in twenty-five is a *synaesthete*; it seems to run in families, is more common in women than in men, and occurs more often than you might expect in left-handers. No one knows why. The word is from the Greek for 'with' and 'sensation' and is related to *anaesthesia* and *anaesthetics,* which are concerned with taking the sensation away.

Synapse c) Part of the nervous system, the junction between two nerve cells across which messages have to pass: breakdown of the synapses is thought to be a major factor in some forms of dementia. From the Greek for 'junction with'.

Syncopation c) The 'offbeat' rhythm used in jazz, when something that should naturally be a weak beat is made strong and vice versa. The word is also an alternative to *syncope* (pronounced *sin-co-pea*), which means loss of consciousness or, in grammar, omitting letters from the middle of a word, as when we say *choc'late* or *cam'ra*. It's all Greek in origin, from a word meaning to strike or cut off. Ensuring several things happen at the same time is *synchronization* (as in 'let's *synchronize* our watches', often heard in spoof gangster and spy films).

Synergy c) Working together. *Ergon* is the Greek for work, as in *energy,* where the *en-* means something like *in* and implies an inbuilt, innate force. With *synergy,* the idea is that things work much better when everyone pulls together – the whole is greater than the sum of the parts, in other words. An ecclesiastical council is a *synod*.

Synthetic a) Artificial, produced by a chemical process, as in *a synthetic material* such as nylon or Lycra. Related to grammatical structure is *syntactical*, the adjective derived from *syntax*.

That's not what I meant

There are many words we tend to misuse. Contrary to popular belief:

- *disinterested* doesn't mean bored (although so many people use it as if it did that this may be a losing battle). *Uninterested* means bored; *disinterested* means impartial, not affected by business *interests* or the opportunity to make a profit. If you ever find yourself on trial for something, you'll want a jury that is *disinterested* (has no axe to grind and with any luck won't find you guilty unless you are) rather than *uninterested* (doesn't care whether you're guilty or not).
- *enormity* is not about size – it doesn't mean *enormousness*. It's to do with evilness, or at the very least outrageousness: *the enormity of his actions shocked even the most hardened cynics.*
- *fulsome* is not a compliment. *Fulsome praise* is extravagant, over-the-top praise, unlikely to be sincere.
- *scarify* doesn't mean *scare*. For that you want *terrify* or *horrify*. Or indeed *scare*. *Scarifying* is something that gardeners do to soil or to seeds, not intended to be frightening.

Words from Shakespeare

Shakespeare probably didn't invent many of the words and expressions that are credited to him, but he was the first person to put them on paper in works that have come down to us. It's because of him that we have *assassination*, used by Macbeth with reference to the murder of King Duncan. Oddly, there is no mention of assassins or assassination in *Julius Caesar*, but that play gives us *gusty*, when Cassius speaks of a *raw and gusty day* – not necessarily something you'd expect in a play about Ancient Rome.

So here are some more words for which we have to thank the Bard.

Academe a) A spiny shrub b) A wood used in furniture-making
c) The world of learning

Auspicious a) Able to be heard clearly b) Favourable
c) Questionable

Besmirch a) To dirty b) To plead c) To request in advance

Castigate a) To chatter b) To fortify c) To scold or punish

Consanguineous a) Agreeable b) Closely related c) Easy to see

Dauntless a) Dangerous b) Intrepid c) Unstained

Equivocal a) Ambiguous b) Carrying equal weight c) Harmonious

Frugal a) Frustrating b) Not expensive c) Sulky

Impede a) To accuse b) To endanger c) To obstruct

Lustrous a) Desirous b) Pleasant-tasting c) Radiant

Multitudinous a) Having many different purposes b) Having many children c) Very numerous

New-fangled a) Excessively modern b) Newly minted, as in a coin c) Recently completed

Pageantry a) A poem in praise of the dead b) Spectacular display c) Worshipping many gods

Pedantical a) Hanging downwards b) Of a monument, supported on a base c) Overly concerned with detail

Reclusive a) Lying face down b) Pointing backwards c) Solitary

Refractory a) Easily broken b) Obstinate c) Pleasantly different

Sanctimonious a) Affectedly pious b) Obsessed with hygiene c) Sacred

Scuffle a) To fight in a disorderly manner b) To sink c) To steal

Swagger a) To spend wastefully b) To walk arrogantly c) To wrap up tightly

Unmitigated a) Heedless b) Unproven c) Very intense

Answers

~

Academe c) The world of learning. From *Love's Labour's Lost*: the king and his courtiers have agreed to shun the company of women and spend three years in contemplative study; they plan that their court *shall be a little Academe*. The word was originally more or less interchangeable with *academy*, meaning a place of learning; now it is more often used to refer to the academic community, a world devoted to scholarship. The rather pompous expression *the groves of Academe* comes from the fact that Plato's original Academy in Athens was based in a garden or grove of trees.

Auspicious b) Favourable, occurring under good *auspices* or omens. Shakespeare used it in both *All's Well That Ends Well* (wishing someone good luck) and *The Tempest* (referring to favourable winds for a journey). In Ancient Rome, an *auspex* (plural *auspices*) was a religious official whose job was to interpret omens to help politicians make decisions or to do things on a lucky day. The omens themselves were also called *auspices*, and if the auspices were favourable it was considered safe to go ahead. Nowadays, *under the auspices* of someone or something means with their patronage, their approval: *the book was published under the auspices of the local historical society*.

Besmirch a) To dirty, discolour or, figuratively, to dim the glow of. Laertes uses this in *Hamlet*, warning his sister Ophelia that Hamlet's love for her may not last: *Perhaps he loves you now; / And now no soil nor cautel* [trick] *doth besmirch / The virtue of his will*. But she should be wary: as a prince, he may have to make a political marriage rather than following his heart. To plead and to request in advance are *to beseech* and *to bespeak* respectively (see *bespoke*, page 71).

Castigate c) To scold or punish severely. From *Timon of Athens*, when Timon, having taken a violent dislike to all humankind, has gone to live in a cave. A friend tells him that if he has done this to *castigate his* *pride*, it is a good thing. Unfortunately, he hasn't, so instead it is rather a disaster.

Consanguineous b) Closely related. Sir Toby Belch uses this in *Twelfth Night*, referring to his relationship with his niece, the Lady Olivia: *Am not I consanguineous? Am I not of her blood?*

Dauntless b) Intrepid, not easily *daunted*. In *Henry VI Part III*, the French king refers to the *dauntless mind* of Margaret, Queen of England, a much more powerful leader than her feeble husband.

Equivocal a) Ambiguous, having more than one equally plausible interpretation. *These sentences … / Being strong on both sides, are equivocal*, says Desdemona's father in *Othello*, debating what to do about his daughter's having married without his permission.

Frugal b) Not expensive or extravagant; meagre, as in *a frugal meal*, which will stop you starving but won't earn any awards for gastronomy. Shakespeare uses it in *The Merry Wives of Windsor*, when Mrs Page, having received an unwanted love letter from Sir John Falstaff, wonders how she can have attracted this man: they have met only a few times and, she says, *I was then frugal of my mirth* – she gave him no encouragement.

Impede c) To obstruct, stand in the way of. Lady Macbeth, learning that the witches have prophesied her husband will become king, wants him to hurry home so that she can *chastise with the valour of my tongue / All that impedes thee from the golden round* – in other words, everything that stops him just grabbing the crown. She also worries that Macbeth's nature is too full of *the milk of human kindness* – another expression for which we have to thank Shakespeare.

Lustrous c) Radiant, shiny: *My sword and yours are kin. Good sparks and lustrous*, says one young soldier to others about to go off to war in *All's Well That Ends Well*.

Multitudinous c) Very numerous, although Shakespeare and other poets also use it to mean vast, with reference to the ocean. Macbeth, having murdered Duncan, despairs of ever getting his hands clean: *This my hand will rather / The multitudinous seas incarnadine, / Making the green one red*. That's a lot of blood – or a very guilty conscience.

New-fangled a) Excessively modern, a disapproving description of something the speaker feels we could do without: *a new-fangled gadget*. It wasn't necessarily disparaging in Shakespeare's day: he uses it in a sonnet to refer to clothes that have been badly refurbished: *Some [glory] in their garments though new-fangled ill.*

Pageantry b) Spectacular display, as in the procession of carriages associated with a royal wedding. From *Pericles, Prince of Tyre*, when a character asks us to imagine *What pageantry, what feats, what shows, / What minstrelsy, and pretty din* have been made to greet the king. It – quite rightly – sounds like a splendid party. As for the other options here, a poem in praise of the dead is a *paean*; worshipping many gods is one definition of *paganism*.

Pedantical c) Overly concerned with detail, often in matters of grammar or in observing petty rules. Nowadays, we tend to prefer *pedantic*, but Shakespeare uses the older form in *Love's Labour's Lost*, when he has the witty Lord Berowne promise to give up *Taffeta phrases, silken terms precise, / Three-pil'd hyperboles, spruce affectation, / Figures pedantical*. *Hyperbole*, by the way, features elsewhere in this book (see page 175).

Reclusive c) Solitary, avoiding other people, particularly by going into religious seclusion. In *Much Ado About Nothing* there is the possibility that, if things don't work out with Hero and Claudio's engagement, she may be concealed *in some reclusive and religious life*.

Refractory b) Obstinate, unmanageable, rebellious. In *Troilus and Cressida*, Hector, in the course of a heated argument over his brother Paris's having abducted Helen, points out that civilized countries have *laws to curb those raging appetites that are / Most disobedient and refractory*.

Sanctimonious a) Affectedly pious. In *Measure for Measure* a minor character is accused of being *like the sanctimonious pirate, that went to sea with the ten commandments, but scrap'd one out of the table*. What is meant is that, however pious that pirate pretended to be, he wasn't going to take much notice of 'Thou shalt not steal'.

Scuffle a) To fight in a disorderly manner or, as a noun, a fight of that sort. In the opening scene of *Antony and Cleopatra*, one of Antony's followers says that, in the past, his general *in the scuffles of great fights* *hath burst the buckles on his breast.* Not any more – Antony is now too busy dallying with Cleopatra, which will of course end in tears.

Swagger b) To walk arrogantly. In *A Midsummer Night's Dream,* the fairy Puck happens upon the craftsmen who are rehearsing a play in the forest and wonders who they are: *What hempen homespuns have we swaggering here?*

Unmitigated c) Very intense, not softened or relieved in any way. *Much Ado About Nothing* again, and the same scene as the *reclusive* quote given a moment ago. Hero's reputation is in tatters because her fiancé Claudio has treated her *with public accusation, uncovered slander, unmitigated rancour.*

CONFUSABLES

premier/premium

These may look similar, but *premier* comes from the Latin for first and *premium* from the Latin for prize. So their meanings are quite distinct. *Premier* means 'first in importance' and is also a title meaning much the same as Prime Minister, used for the heads of provinces in Canada and of states in Australia, among others. A *premiere* (the feminine form) is the first performance of a play, film or the like. A *premium* is an additional price (*there is a premium on seats in the front row*) or a value put on something out of respect (*I put a premium on his advice*). You also pay *insurance premiums* and can buy *premium beers* if you care to spend the extra money for allegedly better quality. But when a newspaper's TV listings recently described Hercule Poirot as *Belgium's premium detective,* they simply got it wrong.

Words from other writers

As with Shakespeare, there may not always be hard evidence of someone inventing a word, but we often have a clear idea of who popularized it. You can give yourself extra points (or a warm pat on the back) if you know where these words came from as well as what they mean.

Arduous a) Hard work b) Passionate c) Steep

Blatant a) Loud b) Obvious c) Trembling

Braggadocio a) Boasting b) A long, drawn-out story c) A love of travel, wanderlust

Chintzy a) Gaudy, trashy b) Prone to weeping c) Trembling

Chortle a) To chuckle b) To eat noisily c) To swallow

Cocoon a) To echo b) To spin silk c) To wrap oneself up for protection

Debauchery a) Corrupt behaviour b) An obvious falsehood c) An open space

Didactic a) Feeble b) Instructive c) Well-meaning

Factoid a) An element that contributes to a result b) An essay c) An unreliable piece of information

Flummox a) To bewilder b) To chew noisily c) To slap

Gallimaufry a) A cold wind b) A jumble c) A swear word

Galumph a) To handle awkwardly b) To hoot c) To walk clumsily

Jubilant a) Disloyal b) Feeling great joy c) Hissing

Pandemonium a) Confusion b) A large van c) A widespread disease

Poetaster a) A bad poet b) A critic c) A slave

Portmanteau word A word that ... a) combines two meanings b) expresses praise or affection c) sounds the same as another

Scrooge a) An incurable optimist b) A miser c) A secretary

Sensuous a) Aesthetically pleasing b) Curvaceous c) Tending to arouse the senses

Serendipity The ability to ... a) keep your head when all about you are losing theirs b) make fortunate discoveries by accident c) navigate accurately but apparently by guess

Witticism a) A clever remark b) A deliberate insult c) A direction that isn't the usual one

Answers

Arduous a) Hard work. Used by Alexander Pope in his *Essay on Criticism* (1711), when he wrote of *those arduous paths* that poets trod in order to achieve excellence.

Blatant b) Obvious in a bad way, as in *a blatant lie* or a politician's *blatant attempt to fool the public*. The word is first found in Edmund Spenser's Elizabethan epic *The Faerie Queene* (1590); the poem contains a character called the Blatant Beast, who personifies the evil done in the world by envy and scandalmongering.

Braggadocio a) Boasting. Another character from Spenser's *Faerie Queene* (see above): Braggadochio [sic] is a boastful, cowardly, ungallant knight – everything that a knight shouldn't be. The name seems to be something that Spenser made up, combining *bragging* with an Italian ending. In various spellings, *braggadocio* came to mean any boastful, swaggering person and is now usually used to mean the boasting itself.

Chintzy a) Gaudy, trashy. *Chintz* is a cotton fabric with bright, usually floral patterns on a pale background, once popular for bed coverings and draperies. The novelist George Eliot (in a letter dated 1851) was the first to use the adjective in a figurative sense, meaning cheap and cheerful but rather tasteless.

Chortle a) To chuckle. Lewis Carroll coined a number of words in his poem 'Jabberwocky' (which appears in *Through the Looking-Glass*, 1871) and this is one of them. Obviously, when you are making words up, you can do what you like, but the suggestion is that this might be a combination of *a chuckle* and *a snort*.

Cocoon c) To wrap oneself up for protection. Mark Twain's *A Tramp Abroad* (1880) contains the first known use of this word as a verb: *We … cocooned ourselves in the proper red blankets*. It's inspired by the much older noun meaning the case in which caterpillars and the larvae of many insects wrap themselves for protection while they metamorphose into their adult form (see *metamorphosis*, page 30).

Debauchery a) Corrupt behaviour. The poet John Milton used this in his pamphlet *An Apology for Smectymnuus* in 1642, coupling it with truanting as examples of bad ways for clerks at a university to spend their time.

Didactic b) Instructive. Another word popularized by Milton: he has it as a noun, meaning a writer whose purpose is to instruct rather than to entertain. Nowadays, it's usually an adjective, describing such a person, or their speech or writing, or their manner of delivering an opinion: informative, but not much fun.

Factoid c) An unreliable piece of information. This was a definite coinage – by the novelist and journalist Norman Mailer. In his biography of Marilyn Monroe published in 1973, he defined *factoids* as *facts which have no existence before appearing in a magazine or newspaper, creations which are not so much lies as a product to manipulate emotion in the Silent Majority.* In other words, pieces of information that are so often repeated that they become widely believed, despite the lack of evidence to support them.

An element that contributes to a result is a *factor*.

Flummox a) To bewilder. In Charles Dickens' *Pickwick Papers* (1837), Mr Pickwick is being sued by his landlady for breach of promise. Another character expresses the opinion that, if he doesn't prove an alibi, *he'll be what the Italians call reg'larly flummoxed*. There's no suggestion in modern dictionaries that the word is of Italian origin; it's more likely to derive from an English regional dialect.

Gallimaufry b) A jumble, from a French word for a stew. This is Edmund Spenser again (see *blatant* and *braggadocio*, above). He was the first to use the word in its current figurative sense when, in 1579, he complained about people bringing French and Italian words into English and making the language *a gallimaufray* [sic] *or hodgepodge of all other speeches*. Some would say that this hodgepodge was part of English's charm, but clearly Spenser thought otherwise.

Galumph c) To walk clumsily. Another word from 'Jabberwocky' (see *chortle*, above). The poem's hero, having slain the monstrous Jabberwock, took its head and *went galumphing back*. Carroll's meaning included a feeling of joy – the word may be a combination of *gallop* and *triumph*. But nowadays, *galumphing* is usually just heavy-footed and awkward.

Jubilant b) Feeling great joy, particularly if you express it with celebratory noise and song. Milton used it in *Paradise Lost* (1667), referring to an occasion when *the bright Pomp ascended jubilant* [to Heaven]. It's related to *jubilee*, the observance of a special anniversary, which also crops up in *Paradise Lost*, but was already an established word.

Pandemonium a) Confusion. More Milton, more *Paradise Lost*: he coined the word to denote the place where all (*pan-*) the demons lived. It came to mean a place of wickedness or noisy confusion and nowadays usually denotes the confusion itself. A large van is a *pantechnicon* and a widespread disease a *pandemic*.

Poetaster a) A bad poet. Coined by the scholar Erasmus in 1521, this was used by Ben Jonson as the title of a satirical play in 1601 and took off from there.

Portmanteau word a) A word that combines two meanings. Back to Lewis Carroll (see *chortle* and *galumph*, above), this is Humpty Dumpty explaining 'Jabberwocky' to Alice. The first line of the poem contains the word *slithy*, which he says means *'lithe and slimy' … You see it's like a portmanteau – there are two meanings packed up into one word*. A portmanteau was a sort of suitcase, hinged so that it opened into two compartments, as anyone who did any travelling in Carroll's time would have understood.

Scrooge b) A miser. In Dickens' *A Christmas Carol* (1843), Ebenezer Scrooge is the curmudgeon (see page 158) who hates Christmas; his name has passed into the language to convey anyone who dislikes spending money and says, 'Bah! Humbug!' in response to anything other people enjoy.

Sensuous a) Aesthetically pleasing. Apparently coined by Milton in an essay of 1641 to make a distinction with *sensual*, which meant pleasing to the senses and particularly to the sexual appetite. Strictly speaking, the two words retain these separate meanings, but they are often confused.

Serendipity b) The ability to make fortunate discoveries by accident. One of those rare words – like *pandemonium*, above – about whose origins we can be specific. In a letter to a friend written in 1754, the Gothic novelist Horace Walpole claimed to have come across it in a Persian fairy-tale called *The Three Princes of Serendip*, in which the princes of the title were always making pleasant discoveries. It's more or less certain that Walpole was making this up and had invented the word himself.

Witticism a) A clever remark. A *portmanteau word* (see above) coined in 1677 by the poet and critic John Dryden, combining *wit* and *criticism*.

On the market

The Ancient Greek word for a marketplace was *agora* – a public open space where people could assemble and which was likely to be crowded. The Latin equivalent was the *forum*, and in Rome the forum became the focus of political, religious and social life: there were lots of temples there, as well as the Senate House and the Rostrum from which speeches were made. So all sorts of discussions went on in the *forum* (as they do today in online equivalents) and it's from here that we get the word *forensic*, as in *forensic science* and *forensic medicine* – to do with courts and the law.

The Greeks can't have enjoyed public debate as much as the Romans, because the words we've inherited from their marketplace are *agoraphobia*, a fear of open and crowded spaces, and its related adjective *agoraphobic*.

Strange, but true.

Words of joy and sorrow

English has no shortage of words to express different moods, but which of these make you cheerful and which make you feel a bit down in the mouth?

Alacrity a) Harshness b) Liveliness c) Sorrow

Chastened a) Adventurous b) Speedy c) Subdued, submissive

Contrite a) Apologetic b) Controlled c) Corny, hackneyed

Discomfiture a) Embarrassment b) Nosiness c) Punishment

Forlorn a) Impertinent b) Out of date c) Very unhappy

Gratified a) Free of charge b) Irritated c) Pleased

Lachrymose a) Colourless b) Short of money c) Tearful

Lugubrious a) Connected with disease b) Mournful c) Tasteless

Maudlin a) Indirect b) Overly sentimental c) Shiny

Plaintive a) Calm b) Modest c) Sorrowful

Plethora a) An aptitude b) A large amount c) A shortage

Prodigious a) Skilful b) Wasteful c) Wonderful

Querulous a) Complaining b) Inquiring c) Peculiar

Ribald a) Cheerfully obscene b) Loud c) Miserly

Sanguine a) Bloodthirsty b) Feeble c) Optimistic

Scintillating a) Animated b) Overly romantic c) Spiteful

Sinecure a) A bad deed b) An easy job c) An incurable disease

Sprightly a) Depressed b) Lively and merry c) Thoughtless

Sumptuous a) Brief and to the point b) Horrific c) Magnificent

Answers

Alacrity b) Liveliness, briskness and cheerful enthusiasm, all rolled into one: if you accept an invitation *with alacrity*, it's obvious that yes, please, you'd *really* like to come.

Chastened c) Subdued, submissive, having been scolded or punished. Nothing to do with *chasteness* or *chastity*, this comes from the Latin for to punish and is related to *castigate*.

Contrite a) Apologetic, repentant, sorry for something you've done. There's also a theological sense (*an act of contrition*), meaning repenting of a past sin and resolving not to do it again. Something that is controlled may be *constrained*, while something corny or hackneyed is *trite*.

Discomfiture a) Embarrassment, confusion, with a suggestion of being caught in the act. It comes from an Old French word meaning to defeat in battle and can still have a military sense in English: *Montgomery's prowess in desert warfare led to Rommel's discomfiture*.

Forlorn c) Very unhappy, feeling as if you have been abandoned. Applied to an emotion or an action, it can also mean desperate: *a forlorn hope* or *a forlorn attempt to reach the summit*. *Lovelorn* – suffering from an unrequited passion that makes you miserable – comes from the same Old English word, meaning lost.

Gratified c) Pleased, satisfied, the way you feel if you have done something well and been rewarded or complimented for it: *I was gratified that the committee liked my suggestions, as I had put a lot of thought into them*. Free of charge is *gratis*.

Lachrymose c) Tearful, given to (probably excessive) weeping. This is an unsympathetic word – a *lachrymose person* is likely to prompt you to pass them a Kleenex and suggest they pull themselves together, rather than to put an arm round them and offer them a cup of tea.

Lugubrious b) Mournful, particularly in voice or appearance. A slightly comical word: a bloodhound, with its wrinkled face and drooping ears, could be described as having *a lugubrious expression*.

Maudlin b) Overly sentimental, probably tearful (see *lachrymose*, above) and quite possibly drunk. Derived from the name of the New Testament character Mary Magdalene, who, although associated with vices other than drunkenness, is often depicted in medieval art as weeping in penitence for her sins.

Plaintive c) Sorrowful, expressing grief. As with *querulous* (below), there's a suggestion of whining and self-pity about this word.

Plethora b) A large amount, but in a bad way. An *abundance* is pleasant, just enough to be luxurious; a *plethora* has gone a step too far. There's a feeling of excess (*a plethora of tequila* will give you a hangover) and of making it hard to make a choice (*a plethora of advice* is simply baffling).

Prodigious c) Wonderful, like a *prodigy* – someone, often a child, of extraordinary talent. If it's describing a thing rather than a person, *prodigious* means amazing, perhaps because of its size or its abundance, and usually in a good way. Wasteful is *prodigal*.

Querulous a) Complaining, in an unreasonable, whining way. The implication with *querulous* is that you are acting out of self-pity rather than because you have any real reason to be upset. You can be *a querulous person* or speak in *a querulous tone of voice*. Or, very possibly, both.

Ribald a) Cheerfully obscene, as in *a ribald remark*, introducing something about sex into the conversation. This isn't an unpleasant word: whereas *lasciviousness* (see page 153), *obscenity* and *pornography* are deplorable, *ribaldry* is likely to be rather fun.

Sanguine c) Optimistic, from the Latin for blood. Medieval medicine identified four 'humours' or fluids (blood, phlegm and black and yellow bile) that needed to be in balance for the body to be healthy. A surplus or lack of any of these humours affected both health and mood. Having plenty of blood meant you were ruddy of complexion and cheerful of temperament, and it's the latter meaning that *sanguine* has retained. If you had too much black bile, by the way, you were *melancholic* (sad), the first part of which comes from the Greek for black and is connected with *melatonin*, the hormone that the body produces at night-time and that helps you to sleep.

Scintillating a) Animated, sparkling, as in *a scintillating conversation*, one that is both entertaining and intellectually stimulating. A *scintilla* can be a spark or sparkle (which is what its Latin source means), but more usually it refers to a tiny amount, a jot: *there wasn't a scintilla of enthusiasm in her voice as she answered the phone.*

Sinecure b) An easy job, from the Latin for 'without care' or 'without anyone to look after'. You're paid to do it, but there isn't much to do.

Sprightly b) Lively and merry, like a *sprite* or elfin creature. You might indulge in *a sprightly dance* if the music was suitably light-hearted, or be in *a sprightly mood* if exams were over and the sun was shining.

Sumptuous c) Magnificent, extravagant and probably expensive. A stage musical might be *a sumptuous production*, with lots of scene changes, fancy lighting and spectacular dancing; such a production would almost certainly have *sumptuous costumes*, too.

And what do you do?

———— ∾ ————

Here are some possible answers to that question frequently asked by royalty or by strangers at a party; how many of these occupations do you recognize? (Note that – for financial, moral or historical reasons – not all of them would be recommended by a twenty-first-century careers adviser.)

Amanuensis a) A concubine b) A secretary c) A skilled labourer

Apothecary a) A dispenser of drugs b) An editor c) A town crier

Chiropodist A therapist who … a) manipulates the spine b) reads the palm c) treats the feet

Croupier Someone employed in … a) a casino b) a dental surgery c) a racing stable

Curator Someone employed in … a) a fire station b) a museum c) a police station

Dilettante a) An embroiderer b) A sculptor c) Someone who dabbles in a number of subjects

Docent a) A lecturer b) A lion-tamer c) A paramedic

Ethnologist An expert in … a) insects b) people and races c) word origins

Evangelist a) An advocate of a cause b) A fortune-teller c) A valuer of jewellery

Footpad a) A maker or mender of shoes b) A robber c) A servant

Gumshoe a) A detective b) An interior decorator c) A sports teacher

Hussar a) A cavalryman b) An early form of cheerleader c) A housewife

Lexicographer A compiler of … a) crossword puzzles b) dictionaries c) quizzes

Milliner a) A grinder of corn b) A maker of hats c) A part-time soldier

Ophthalmologist A medical practitioner specializing in diseases of … a) the digestive system b) the ear c) the eye

Pugilist a) A boxer b) A breeder of dogs c) A glass-blower

Sommelier a) An accountant b) A hypnotherapist c) A wine waiter

Stenographer a) An expert in dinosaurs b) A shorthand typist c) A weather forecaster

Tribune a) An official b) A member of a group of three directors of a company c) Someone who leads the service at a funeral

Vigilante a) A self-appointed guard b) A speechmaker c) A winemaker

Answers

Amanuensis b) A secretary – in Ancient Rome it denoted a slave employed to take down dictation or to copy manuscripts.

Apothecary a) A dispenser of drugs – the medieval equivalent of a pharmacist or chemist.

Chiropodist c) A therapist who treats the feet, particularly getting rid of corns, bunions and the like. The person who manipulates the spine is a *chiropractor*.

Croupier a) Someone employed in a casino, to deal cards, spin the roulette wheel, collect stakes and – at a pinch – pay out winnings.

Curator b) Someone employed in a museum or art gallery, in charge of their collection(s) or of putting together a special exhibition.

Dilettante c) Someone who dabbles in a number of subjects, generally the arts, without having a professional interest or reaching a professional standard in any of them.

Docent a) A lecturer at some US universities, not on the salaried staff but recognized as qualified to teach on a specific subject. From the Latin for to learn or to teach, and therefore related to *doctor*.

Ethnologist b) An expert in people and races. The study of insects is *entomology* and of word origins *etymology*.

Evangelist a) An advocate of a cause. Originally used of the Christian doctrine – the writers of the biblical Gospels (Matthew, Mark, Luke and John) are known as the Evangelists – but now applicable to any cause that involves 'spreading the word': *a number of evangelists for home baking have emerged from recent television programmes.*

Footpad b) A robber who held up travellers. A highwayman traditionally worked on horseback, a footpad on foot.

Gumshoe a) A detective, particularly a rather downtrodden private detective. So called because he (and it was usually a he) moved around stealthily, as if wearing soft rubber (or gum) shoes that didn't make a noise as he crept up on you.

Hussar a) A cavalryman. Although there is still a regiment known as the Queen's Royal Hussars, the term is largely historical: in the seventeenth and eighteenth centuries there were hussar regiments all over Europe, renowned for their elegant uniforms as much as for their horsemanship.

Lexicographer b) A compiler of dictionaries. Dr Samuel Johnson, the famous eighteenth-century lexicographer, defined the word as, among other things, 'a harmless drudge'.

Milliner b) A maker of hats. From the Italian city of Milan, once famous for producing women's accessories and knick-knacks of all kinds.

Ophthalmologist c) A medical practitioner specializing in diseases of the eye, as opposed to an *optician* or *optometrist*, who examines the eyes and, if necessary, prescribes spectacles or lenses.

Pugilist a) A boxer, usually a professional one.

Sommelier c) A wine waiter in a restaurant or hotel, usually a senior person with a considerable knowledge of wine. From an old French word for a butler and still pronounced in the French way, so that the ending rhymes with *tea tray* rather than with *beer*.

Stenographer b) A shorthand typist or someone who takes notes, minutes and so on in shorthand. From the Greek for 'narrow writing'.

Tribune a) An official – in ancient Rome, one who protected the interests of the common people; now a champion of public rights, a popular leader. Related to *tribunal*, a court such as *an industrial tribunal*, established to inquire into a specific issue. Reverting to Roman times, a board of three was a *triumvirate*, while someone at a funeral might deliver a *tribute*.

Vigilante a) A self-appointed guard, usually a member of a group or committee that devotes itself to protecting the homes or property in its neighbourhood. From the Latin for staying awake and related to *vigil* and *vigilant*, *vigilante* is often a negative term for people eager to enforce racist or other prejudiced views. Pronounced as four syllables – *vigil-anti*.

Four-letter words

No, not the rude kind. Just a few examples to show that words don't have to be long in order to be interesting.

Acme a) Pain b) A skin complaint c) The peak of achievement

Bane a) A handkerchief b) Something forbidden c) Something that causes distress

Bevy a) A drinking session b) A group c) A tent

Boor a) An ill-mannered person b) A platform c) A tedious task

Coda a) A final part b) An Italian jacket c) Rubbish

Diva a) A backless sofa b) A singer c) A small dog

Ergo a) A disease b) Enthusiasm, impetus c) Therefore

Flux a) Continuous change b) Part of an anchor c) A tube

Gist a) An energetic dance b) The essential point c) Something useful

Glib a) Fluent b) A lamp c) A thick fluid

Hype a) A coma b) Exaggerated publicity c) An illegal drug

Kudu a) An African antelope b) Caribbean magic c) Praise

Nook a) A corner b) A nudge c) A play on words

Pyre a) A church official b) A pile of wood c) A tower

Rime a) A folk song b) Frost c) A tree

Serf a) A grass b) Scum c) A slave

Silo a) A delicate material b) Muddy water c) A storage tower

Trug a) A basket b) A long walk c) A musical instrument

Waft a) To be carried on the air b) To hum or sing quietly c) To waste

Yoke a) A frame b) A joke c) The yellow part of an egg

CONFUSABLES

aural/oral

The Latin *auris* means the ear; *os* (which in the plural becomes *ora*) is the mouth. Thus *aural* is to do with the ear or hearing; *oral* is connected to the mouth or speech. In an *aural/oral exam*, you would expect to listen to the questions and answer them verbally rather than writing anything down; you might also have *an aural examination* if you thought you were going deaf, but visit the dentist for concerns about *oral hygiene*.

Answers

~

Acme c) The peak of achievement, the pinnacle of success. Pain, of course, is *ache* and *acne* is a skin disease.

Bane c) Something that causes distress, as in *he is the bane of my existence* – the person who *really* makes my life a misery. Once upon a time, a *bane* was also a poison, hence the various plants such as *wolf's bane*, alleged to be harmful to or to ward off the animal in question.

Bevy b) A group, originally of young women but now of any gathering – *the usual bevy of teenagers were hanging around the mall*. Also, in the eccentric world of collective nouns, a group of quails or of larks. *Bevvy* with two vs is a slang word for a drinking session; a small tent might be a *bivvy*, from *bivouac*, a temporary camp.

Boor a) An ill-mannered person, particularly one who is clumsy and insensitive to the feelings of others. A platform on which a coffin rests is a *bier* and a tedious task is a *chore*.

Coda a) A final part, usually in a musical composition but sometimes also the epilogue or afterword to a written work. From the Italian for 'tail'.

Diva b) A singer, the principal female in an opera company. Also known as a *prima donna*, Italian for 'first lady'. Both these terms can be used away from the world of opera to denote a woman who is demanding, unreasonable and prone to losing her temper spectacularly if things don't go her way. A backless sofa is a *divan*.

Ergo c) Therefore. This is simply the Latin word, to be used in English when you have set out the reasons for an argument and are about to draw a conclusion: *there were no fingerprints on the gun, ergo someone wiped them off after pulling the trigger*. There is a disease of cereals called *ergot*.

Four-letter words

Flux a) Continuous change, a flowing back and forth. Often *a state of flux*, as in *his emotions had been in a state of flux ever since he received the letter; he couldn't decide whether he was excited or horrified.* Part of an anchor (or part of a whale's tail, with the same shape as an anchor) is a *fluke*, while a tube to carry smoke out of a chimney is a *flue*.

Gist b) The essential point, the substance: *you can read the whole article later, but the gist of it is that the project needs more money.* Something useful might figuratively be *grist to your mill*; *grist* is literally grain that needs to be or has just been ground.

Glib a) Fluent, easy of speech, especially with the intent to deceive or to gloss over unpleasant details: *he had a glib explanation for being late, but we suspected he had been up to no good.* In old-fashioned slang, a lamp might be a *glim*; a dollop of thick fluid is a *glob*.

Hype b) Exaggerated publicity: *despite all the hype, I thought the film was rubbish. Hype* can also be a verb – *to hype something up* is to promote it wildly, without necessarily sticking to the truth.

Kudu a) An African antelope with a striped body and twisted horns. Caribbean magic is *voodoo* and praise is *kudos* (see pages 149 and 164).

Nook a) A corner or secluded place – a cosy spot to which to retreat. Often found in the expression *every nook and cranny*, where a *cranny* is a chink or crevice in a wall. So *to search every nook and cranny* is to look absolutely everywhere. An *inglenook* is another cosy place, the corner of a fireplace, with *ingle* being an old-fashioned word for fireplace or hearth.

Pyre b) A pile of wood on which a corpse is cremated. From the Greek for a hearth or fire. The prefix *pyro-* comes from the same source and is thus connected with fire, as in a *pyromaniac*, someone with a passion for lighting fires, and *pyrotechnics*, fireworks or a brilliant display in a piece of music.

Rime b) Frost, specifically 'frost formed by the rapid freezing of supercooled water droplets in cloud or fog when they make contact with a cold object', as opposed to *hoar frost*, which is … oh, something different. But still cold.

Serf c) A slave. In medieval Europe, a *serf* was bound to the land (which of course he didn't own or make any money from) and could be passed on from one owner to the next if the land was sold.

Silo c) A storage tower in which to keep *silage*, a crop harvested for fodder.

Trug a) A basket – the long, low style used in gardening, for carrying flowers or tools. A long, tiring walk is a *trudge* or a *trek*.

Waft a) To be carried on the air. A gentle word, this – a pleasant scent is likely to *waft* in the window if you have planted, say, a lilac outside.

Yoke a) A frame, such as is used to join two oxen together so that they can pull the same plough. The yellow part of an egg is pronounced the same but spelled *yolk*.

Five-letter words

Longer (and every bit as polite) as the four-letter words in the previous quiz. Still quite short, though …

Aloof a) Distant and cold in manner b) Strongly contrasting c) Stupid

Eclat a) Applause b) A heroic deed c) Showy success

Feint a) A distraction b) A failure c) A shiver

Filch a) To pamper b) To squelch, move through mud c) To steal

Gloss a) An explanation b) A shiny fabric c) One of the vocal cords

Helix a) A gas b) A spiral shape c) A wild cat

Inure a) To add a hard outer coating b) To cause to become used to c) To insult

Laity a) Fat b) A link c) Not the clergy

Lithe a) Eager b) Flexible c) Pale, unhealthy-looking

Macho a) Dirty b) Muddled c) Overtly masculine

Mêlée a) A brawl b) A piece of pottery c) A type of stew

Mores a) Customs b) Funeral arrangements c) Second helpings

Opine a) To express an opinion b) To long for c) To resist

Quaff a) To drink enthusiastically b) To laugh loudly c) To wear

Quirk a) A feeling b) A gesture c) A peculiarity

Salvo a) A burst of fire b) A sudden leap c) A toast

Satyr a) A lack, a shortfall b) A lecherous man c) A type of tree

Staid a) Dignified and well-behaved b) Obvious c) Overdue

Sully a) To dirty b) To misbehave c) To trample

Vapid a) Boring b) Over too quickly c) Unhealthily thin

Answers

~

Aloof a) Distant and cold in manner, giving the impression that whatever is going on is of no interest and rather beneath you.

Eclat c) Showy success, from a French word meaning glamour, brilliance or sparkle – impressive but unlikely to last long. If it doesn't have a capital letter, it should have an acute accent (*éclat*); and, because it's French, you don't pronounce the *t*.

Feint a) A distraction, originally in fencing or boxing, when you look as if you are going to lunge or punch in one direction, deceive your opponent and then thrust your sword or your fist somewhere completely different. Pronounced *faint*.

Filch c) To steal, in a small way – you'd *filch* the petty cash rather than the Crown Jewels. If you were that way inclined, of course.

Gloss a) An explanation, the sort of note an editor might put in the margin to clarify an obscure word, or that you might use to spell out what you meant if you were quoting someone else. Related to *glossary*, but nothing to do with shiny paint.

Helix b) A spiral shape, more specifically 'a curve that lies on a cylinder or cone, at a constant angle to the line segments making up the surface'. To put it in more approachable terms, the shell of a snail takes the form of a helix, and DNA occurs in a double helix, with two strands of molecules twining round each other.

Inure b) To cause to become used to. That may sound like an odd definition and the word isn't often used in this active way. More common is the adjectival *inured*, meaning used to or even resigned to: *don't bother to apologize. I am completely inured to your bad manners.*

Laity c) Not the clergy – derived from the Greek for *people*. In some sectors of the Christian Church, *lay preachers* or *lay readers* are allowed to lead certain services, although they are not fully ordained clerics; the word also applies to those who are not experts in whatever field is under discussion, whether it is the Church, the law, advertising or building. The point is that the *layman* or *laywoman* doesn't have specialist knowledge, so they may need you to translate technical language into *layman's* (or *lay*) terms.

Lithe b) Flexible, supple – a word you might apply to a dancer, a gymnast or anyone else with a slim and bendy figure.

Macho c) Overtly masculine. This is the ordinary Spanish word for male, but in English it has negative overtones: *a macho man* is likely to be muscular and enjoy showing off his fitness; *macho attitudes* might include unwillingness to do the ironing and a tendency to become aggressive after a few beers.

Mêlée a) A brawl, particularly a confused one with fists flying. The word is related to *medley* and comes from the French for mix; you don't need to include the accents if you don't want to, but with or without them it's pronounced *mell-eh*.

Mores a) Customs, conventions, from the Latin word that also gave us *moral*. Pronounced as two syllables (*more-ehs*), it's used more in sociology than in everyday speech: the *mores* of a society are a fundamental part of how it works.

Opine a) To express an opinion, and from the same Latin root as *opinion*. It's a slightly disapproving word – if you say that someone *opined that the country was going to the dogs*, you'd be implying that they were being pompous and that you didn't necessarily agree with them.

Quaff a) To drink enthusiastically or in one draught. Usually alcohol. You could, at a pinch, quaff a large glass of water if you were extremely thirsty, but you can't really quaff coffee. Partly because it's too hot, partly because it sounds silly. Pronounced to rhyme with *off*.

Quirk c) A peculiarity in a person's character: *it was one of his quirks that he wouldn't go out without his velvet jacket, no matter how hot it was*. Often found in the expression *a quirk of fate*, one of those strange things that you can do nothing about: *my meeting her in the park was a quirk of fate – we hadn't planned to fall in love again*.

Salvo a) A burst of fire, both literally with gunfire and metaphorically with questions, complaints or verbal abuse.

Satyr b) A lecherous man. In Greek mythology, the Satyrs were the part-human, part-goat-like companions of Dionysus, the god of wine, described as 'lustful and full of revelry'. In modern use, there's no suggestion of revelry – a satyr is an unpleasant man with predatory instincts.

Staid a) Dignified, well-behaved and perhaps just a little bit boring. It's related to *stay*, so a staid person is settled in their ways, unenthusiastic about moving with the times.

Sully a) To dirty – usually used of a reputation rather than of something more tangible, like a football shirt. It's unpleasant: *a sullied reputation* is unlikely ever to be clean again.

Vapid a) Boring, lifeless – *vapid conversation* will put you to sleep if you have to listen to too much of it. Originally used of wine and other drinks, it meant tasteless and flat when it was supposed to be sparkling.

Six-letter words

Getting a bit longer …

Abject a) Argumentative b) Hateful c) Submissive

Albino a) Colourless b) Mountainous c) Painful

Apogee a) A defence b) The highest point c) A type of sword

Cachet a) Distinction b) A hiding place c) A tie

Cajole a) To coax b) To grumble c) To scold

Craven a) Black b) Cowardly c) Having a hearty appetite

Curfew a) A collector's item b) A regulation c) A scarf

Dictum a) A basket b) An order c) A saying

Effete a) Decadent b) Flowing c) Powerful

Eschew a) To avoid b) To comfort c) To protect

Galore a) Heavy-footed b) In abundance c) Poetic

Lacuna a) A body of water b) A gap c) A hiccup

Litany a) A day bed b) A joke c) A tedious speech

Mayhem a) Chaos b) Permission c) A springtime festival

Minion a) A reduction b) A servant c) A small cake

Penury a) An illusion b) A near miss c) Poverty

Rubric a) Bad temper b) Instructions c) A red dye

Schism a) A division b) A parody c) Thriftiness

Solace a) Comfort b) Honesty c) Loneliness

Zenith a) Enthusiasm b) The highest point c) Women's quarters

CONFUSABLES

principal/principle

Principal means 'main', as in the *principal violinist* in an orchestra, the head teacher of a school or the person for whom an agent acts: *I am authorized to offer you $100,000 – I can't go further than that without consulting my principal.* *Principle* is a standard of conduct or a strongly held belief: *a woman of principle* can't be flattered or bribed into doing something of which she disapproves; she may indeed *object on principle* to whatever you are suggesting. You can also have an agreement *in principle*: that's one in which you are happy with the broad terms but still have to sort out the fine print.

Answers

~

Abject c) Submissive, grovelling – offering *an abject apology* means you are deeply ashamed of yourself. *Abject* can also mean contemptible – *an abject liar* tells particularly appalling lies; or it can mean utter, absolute – someone in *abject poverty* genuinely can't afford to eat.

Albino a) Colourless: lacking the pigment melanin that gives the skin, hair and eyes their colour. An *albino person* (or an *albino*) is likely to have white hair, very pale skin and pink-rimmed eyes; animals and plants can be *albino* too. From the Latin for white. Unlike some other technical terms in this section, the word isn't generally used in any figurative sense.

Apogee b) The highest point. An astronomical term meaning the point in its orbit when the moon is at its greatest distance from the Earth, but used more freely to mean a climax or peak of achievement: *with hindsight, commentators realized that the financial sector had reached its apogee – a crash was bound to follow.* In this looser sense, *apogee* means much the same as *zenith* (see below), but is in less common use.

Cachet a) Distinction, prestige. A French word, so the middle sound is soft (*sh*) and the *t* isn't pronounced. Like *je ne sais quoi, cachet* is often preceded by *a certain*: *her presence added a certain cachet to the party – you don't often see a duchess in your local pub.* A hiding place is a *cache*.

Cajole a) To coax, wheedle, pester in order to get your own way – *oh, pleease can I go? Pretty please? Pleease let me.* That's cajoling.

Craven b) Cowardly, in an *abject* (see above), shrinking way: *he was terrified of new people and new experiences; in fact, he had a craven attitude to life in general.*

Curfew b) A regulation – originally, in medieval Europe, one that stated that, at a certain hour, fires must be extinguished (the French *couvre-feu* means 'cover fire'). That meant that any burning lights, lanterns or candles must also be put out, effectively imposing a black-out and keeping people confined to their own homes. Nowadays, it's not the darkness so much as the being at home that is important: a teenager might have *a ten o'clock curfew* on a school night – be home by ten or else – while a totalitarian regime might *impose a curfew* on its citizens after dark, so that no subversive meetings could take place. A collector's item is a *curio*.

Dictum c) A saying, a maxim: *it was a dictum of my father's that no one could play a decent game of bridge without a dry martini beside them.* More personal and less bossy than a *diktat* (see page 91), to which it is loosely related.

Effete a) Decadent, weak – used of a person, a society or an artistic movement that has lost its vigour and become ineffective, worn out and possibly immoral: *the effete race of former Empire-builders.* Sometimes used as if it meant *effeminate*, but it shouldn't be – *effete* comes from a Latin word meaning 'having brought forth young and now exhausted by it' (it's related to *foetus*). Hardly the same as a man or boy 'displaying characteristics regarded as typical of a woman', which is one dictionary's definition of *effeminate*.

Eschew a) To avoid, to keep clear of a person or a thing: *I have chosen to eschew his company* is a pompous way of saying you don't want to be seen dead with him.

Galore b) In abundance, as in the 1940s novel and film *Whisky Galore!* or expressions such as *there were poppies galore growing by the side of the road.* Note that *galore* comes immediately *after* the word it's describing: you can't have *galore whisky* or *a galore of poppies*.

Lacuna b) A gap, particularly a missing section in an old manuscript, though the word also has various technical meanings in botany and anatomy. It can be used more generally, though it may sound a bit pretentious: *there were lacunae in his argument that showed he hadn't thought the matter through.* Note the Latin plural (*-ae*), which adds to the pretentiousness. A body of water may be a *lagoon* (or, of course, a *lake*).

Litany c) A tedious speech. Strictly speaking, in the Christian Church, a form of prayer in which the congregation gives an unvarying response. Thus, by extension, any repetitive recital or list: *there was the usual litany of complaints about noisy neighbours, litter and vandalism.*

Mayhem a) Chaos, noisy confusion: *the chairman lost control of the meeting and the Q & A session descended into mayhem*. Nothing to do with the month of May, but related to *maim*.

Minion b) A servant or an unimportant underling or hanger-on. Often used jokingly, in a mock-superior way: *if I can't do it myself, I'll get one of my minions on to it*.

Penury c) Poverty of a particularly drastic kind. Often used to make an exaggerated point: *if you go on buying new shoes we'll be reduced to penury*.

Rubric b) Instructions, as at the beginning of a puzzle or game to explain the rules, or at the head of an exam paper, telling candidates how many questions to answer. It comes from the Latin for 'red ochre', because such instructions, particularly in the early Church where the concept originated, were traditionally written in red.

Schism a) A division between two parts of the same group: *the issue caused a schism within the party*. In ecclesiastical history there have been various *schisms* over doctrine in the Christian Church, most famously the Great Schism of 1054, which separated what is now the Catholic Church from the Eastern Orthodox.

Solace a) Comfort, particularly in times of trouble. Jane Austen's *Pride and Prejudice* has this famous description of Mrs Bennet: *The business of her life was to get her daughters married; its solace was visiting and news*.

Zenith b) The highest point. Specifically, in astronomy, the point on the celestial sphere vertically above an observer; more generally, the peak of someone's achievements: *That year was the zenith of my career; I never felt so fulfilled again*. And see *apogee* (above). The women's quarters in some Muslim and Hindu homes are the *zenana*.

Seven-letter words

The words may be longer, but are they any more familiar?

Abreast a) Bored b) Curt c) Informed

Bespoke a) Dirty b) Made to order c) Opinionated

Bibelot a) An apron b) A small cup c) A trinket

Buoyant a) Cheerful b) Fresh c) Indiscreet

Coterie a) A form of embroidery b) Gossip c) A small group

Cursory a) Angry b) Direct c) Quick, superficial

Denizen a) A hermit or recluse b) A prisoner c) A resident

Igneous a) Humiliating b) Imperfect c) Related to fire

Inkling a) A child's garment b) A short letter c) A slight suggestion

Kumquat a) A fruit b) A position in tai chi c) A warehouse

Macabre a) Cunning b) Enormous c) Gruesome

Maestro a) A dignified piece of music b) A distinguished musician c) A form of pasta

Malaise a) Clumsiness b) Ill will c) Unease

Oblique a) At an angle b) Disgraceful c) Obedient

Pelagic a) Covered with fur b) Dangerous c) To do with the open sea

Phoneme a) An early cell phone b) A legendary bird c) A unit of sound

Pyrrhic a) Bad-tempered b) Golden c) Not worth the effort

Roulade a) A dish served in the form of a roll b) A gambling game c) A merry-go-round

Traduce a) To make advances to b) To speak ill of c) To translate

Yeshiva a) A holy book b) A school c) A skullcap

⟨ CONFUSABLES ⟩

reign/rein

Two simple enough words that are increasingly confused. *Reigning* is what a monarch does, ruling over a kingdom. *Reins* are the leather straps used to control a horse or a small child, and *to rein someone in* is (literally or figuratively) to pull on those reins in order to hold them back. You can't *reign someone in* – it's meaningless. Or just plain wrong.

Answers

Abreast c) Informed, up to speed: *we went for a coffee before the meeting so that I could bring her abreast of the latest developments*. Also, literally, alongside each other: *we were walking three abreast* means that there were three of us in a row, all heading in the same direction. Curt, brief and to the point in speech is *abrupt*.

Bespoke b) Made to order, usually of clothing – the opposite of *ready-made* or *off the peg*. Hence *bespoke shoes* or a *bespoke suit*, which you might order from a *bespoke tailor*, one who specializes in that sort of work. *To bespeak* is an old-fashioned word for to order in advance – *I'll write to the hotel to bespeak rooms for us* – and *bespoke* is an adjective formed from this.

Bibelot c) A trinket, an attractive or curious knick-knack. It's a French word, so don't pronounce the *t*.

Buoyant a) Cheerful, able to bounce back from any reversal of fortune. Also, literally, able to float, like the sort of *buoy* that bobs around in the sea to alert ships to obstacles or mooring places. The first syllable is pronounced *boy*.

Coterie c) A small group, a clique or 'in crowd', very much implying that others are excluded: *everyone wanted to be part of the director's coterie, but he encouraged only those who were already good actors*.

Cursory c) Quick, superficial. From the Latin for run and its meaning echoed in the *cursor* that runs over your computer screen: *she gave the minutes no more than a cursory glance, even though I'd asked her to check them carefully*.

Denizen c) A resident, normally of a country of which you are not a native but where you have certain rights. The word can also be applied to a plant or animal that has established itself in a non-native habitat, and may be used in a less formal sense: in F. Scott Fitzgerald's *The Great*

Gatsby, someone is described as *quite a character around New York – a denizen of Broadway*. From the Latin for 'from within'.

Igneous c) Related to fire, used almost exclusively with reference to the sort of rock that is produced by volcanic activity.

Inkling c) A slight suggestion, the tiniest idea: *I had no inkling of what was going on*. Nothing to do with *ink*, this comes from an old word *inkle*, meaning to whisper or hint.

Kumquat a) A fruit, small, round and orange in colour. Originally from China, its name is Cantonese for 'golden orange'.

Macabre c) Gruesome, associated with death: *the macabre sight of the ghost with her head under her arm*. The *danse macabre* or dance of death was an art form in the Middle Ages, with many artists and musicians producing works warning that everyone, rich or poor, noble or otherwise, was united in the journey towards the grave. *Macabre* is a French word, with the emphasis on the second syllable and the last syllable pronounced *brr* rather than *ber* if you want to keep the French tone.

Maestro b) A distinguished musician, often the conductor of an orchestra and often used as a form of address: *Music, maestro, please*. It's the Italian word for master. *Maestoso* is the Italian for majestic, used as an instruction for how to play a piece of music – in this case, a particularly dignified one.

Malaise c) Unease: the feeling of being mildly unwell or a bit depressed, in both cases without being able to pinpoint what is wrong: *I had been suffering from a certain malaise, which the doctor couldn't explain*; or *anxiety over the company's poor results contributed to a general malaise in the office*. Someone who is clumsy is *maladroit* and ill will is *malice*.

Oblique a) At an angle, either literally (an *oblique stroke* looks like this: /) or figuratively, as with *an oblique reference* to, say, a piece of gossip – hinting at it without coming right out and saying it.

Pelagic c) To do with the open sea, often applied to marine life (*the pelagic lifestyle of the whale shark*) or to birds such as albatrosses and petrels that spend most of their time in flight a long way from land.

Phoneme c) A unit of sound that cannot be broken down into smaller parts and is essential for distinguishing between different words: *l*, *s* and *t* are the *phonemes* that differentiate *lend*, *send* and *tend*. The legendary bird is a *phoenix*.

Pyrrhic c) Not worth the effort. From the victory of the Greek general Pyrrhus over the Romans in two battles of the third century BC, in which the losses of the winning side were as great as those of the losers. Pyrrhus is quoted as saying, 'Another victory like this and we are lost.' The adjective *Pyrrhic* is rarely applied to anything other than a victory, but it needn't refer to warfare: it could be a *Pyrrhic victory* if you broke the bank at Monte Carlo but then found yourself barred from the casino. Don't be frightened by the fancy spelling: it's pronounced to rhyme with *lyric*.

Roulade a) A dish served in the form of a roll. Originally this was a slice of meat wrapped round a stuffing; nowadays, the only thing that matters is the concept of wrapping: you can spread cream cheese and spinach on pitta bread and call it a *roulade* as long as you have rolled it up.

Traduce b) To speak ill of, to slander with a view to destroying someone's reputation. From the Latin for to lead across or to disgrace.

Yeshiva b) A school where Jewish children study rabbinical law and the theological text, the Talmud. The Jewish skullcap is a *yarmulke*.

Animal words

We've adopted a number of animal (and bird and insect) names into words whose meanings have drifted away from their zoological sources. Can you tell your doggerel from your catechism?

Bugbear a) Another name for the grizzly bear b) A large beetle c) A source of fear or annoyance

Cat's paw a) A game played with loops of string b) A person exploited by another c) A whip

Cock-a-hoop a) Boastful b) Noisy c) Well dressed

Cowlick a) A meadow flower b) A heap of dung c) A lock of hair

Cry wolf a) To boast about one's bravery b) To pay extravagant compliments c) To raise a false alarm

Gooseflesh a) Another name for *foie gras* b) The material once used to stuff an eiderdown c) A reaction to cold or fright

Hippocampus a) A monster in Greek mythology b) The parade ground on a race course c) Part of the brain

Hogshead a) A monster alleged to frighten naughty children b) A quantity of wine c) A sporting trophy hung on the wall

Horse latitudes a) High latitudes, near the poles b) Low latitudes, near the equator c) Mid-latitudes, somewhere between the two

Kangaroo court a) A court whose findings have no legal standing b) An early Australian stock exchange c) A venue for amateur tennis

Lion's share a) The largest portion b) Long, untidy hair c) A meal consisting entirely of meat

Loan shark Someone who … a) buys up mortgages b) lends money at high rates of interest c) offers attractive odds on a horse race

Monkey puzzle a) An 'enrichment' activity in zoos b) A fern c) A tree

Parrot fashion a) Loudly and showily b) Without stopping c) Without thinking about it

Rhinoplasty a) Having two horns b) A nose job c) A semi-precious stone

Scapegoat a) An escaped prisoner b) Someone to take the blame c) A stupid person

Squirrel away a) To hide b) To run away from danger c) To study conscientiously

Swan song a) The evening equivalent of the 'dawn chorus' b) A final appearance c) A tuneless rendition

Tiger balm a) Calming music b) An Indian tree c) An ointment

White elephant a) A large spider b) A skin complaint c) Something expensive and useless

Answers

~

Bugbear c) A source of fear or annoyance, particularly an irrational one. Also known as a *bugaboo*. Originally a goblin (possibly in the form of a bear) who ate naughty children. The *bug* part is nothing to do with insects but comes from an old word for a monster or bogeyman.

Cat's paw b) A person exploited by another, used as a tool to achieve a particular end. According to an old legend, a monkey once used a cat's paw as a rake to remove roasted chestnuts from a fire. The game played with loops of string is *cat's cradle*, while a *cat-o'-nine-tails* is a sort of whip.

Cock-a-hoop a) Boastful, like a cock crowing in triumph.

Cowlick c) A lock of hair, usually flat against the forehead and looking as if it has been licked by a cow. The meadow flower is a *cowslip* and the heap of dung a *cowpat*.

Cry wolf c) To raise a false alarm. According to Aesop, the Ancient Greek compiler of fables, a shepherd boy, bored with looking after his sheep, thought it would be funny to call out 'Wolf!' and have the villagers rush out to scare the non-existent wolf away. And it was – hilarious, until he had done it once too often. When a wolf did appear, the villagers didn't believe his cries for help, so that the wolf ate the sheep (and in some versions the boy as well). Be warned.

Gooseflesh c) A reaction to cold or fright, when something 'makes your flesh creep'. The body's physical response to these stimuli includes a contraction of certain muscles, giving the skin the appearance of a plucked goose. Or so they say.

Hippocampus c) Part of the brain, so called because in cross-section it looks a bit like a sea horse. The scientific name for a sea horse is *Hippocampus*, from the Greek for – reasonably enough – 'a sea monster that looks like a horse'. The monster in Greek mythology (and indeed in Harry Potter) – part horse, part griffon – is a *hippogriff*, and *hippopotamus* translates as 'river horse'.

Hogshead b) A quantity of wine – 52½ imperial gallons or about 63 US gallons/almost 240 litres. A lot of wine. No one seems quite sure where the name came from: possibly from the shape of the barrel. It's certainly more than you could fit into the average hog's head, even if the idea of drinking from such a receptacle didn't turn your stomach.

Horse latitudes c) Mid-latitudes, somewhere between the two – about 30° north or south, where sailors often came across periods of calm or unpredictable winds. The name may come from the belief that many horses and other animals died aboard ship in these conditions.

Kangaroo court a) A court whose findings have no legal standing, often held by strikers, mutineers or prisoners to pass judgement on one of their peers. Oddly, the term originated not in Australia but in the USA – chosen, perhaps, because this sort of court bounced up when it was needed and then went away again.

Lion's share a) The largest portion, the share that a strong and fierce creature such as a lion would take.

Loan shark b) Someone who lends money at high rates of interest, from the idea of a shark as a merciless predator.

Monkey puzzle c) A tree of the genus *Araucaria*, whose branches curve upwards and bear stiff, sharp leaves, suggesting that even a monkey would have difficulty climbing it, or that once it *was* up it would have difficulty getting down, with all those spikes pointing towards it.

Parrot fashion c) Without thinking about it, repeating something that has been learned without taking in its meaning.

Rhinoplasty b) A nose job, plastic surgery to the nose. *Rhino* comes from the Greek for nose, and the name *rhinoceros* means that the animal's nose has a horn or horns on it.

Scapegoat b) Someone to take the blame, from the biblical story of the goat that was symbolically laden with the sins of the Israelites and sent out into the desert to perish as a symbol of atonement.

Squirrel away a) To hide, to store for future use, in the manner of a squirrel hoarding nuts for the winter. To study conscientiously, or to work hard at any task, might be *to beaver away*.

Swan song b) A final appearance. According to tradition, a dying swan sings a particularly beautiful and moving song; so a human performer's last appearance, whether musical or not, has the same poignancy.

Tiger balm c) An ointment – the brand name of a product originating in eastern Asia, rubbed into the skin to relieve pain, stiffness and so on.

White elephant c) Something expensive and useless. The story goes that the kings of Siam (now Thailand) would make a present of a white elephant to a courtier who had fallen from favour. White elephants weren't allowed to work, so the cost of keeping the elephant would ruin the courtier and leave him no time to plot against the king. Nowadays often used to refer to expensive building projects: *that white elephant in the High Street cost millions to build and it's sitting there empty.*

A slip of the tongue

This book is full of words with strange derivations – see *hippocampus* (page 76) and *scapegoat* (page 77), to name but two – but *shibboleth* may be the oddest of them all. It means a test, a stumbling block, and if you don't know the background it isn't easy to guess it.

It comes from a biblical story that tells us that the Ephraimite people couldn't pronounce the sound *sh*. So an enemy tribe, having defeated them in battle, devised a test to expose any surviving Ephraimites who were trying to conceal their identity. Suspects were asked to say *shibboleth* (which meant an ear of corn); if it came out as *sibboleth*, the game was up. Nowadays, the word generally applies to a social stumbling block – an accent, trick of speech or form of dress that marks you as belonging to a certain, generally unacceptable group: *she clung on to the shibboleths of her class – she wouldn't have been seen dead in a faux fur coat.*

Are you a man ...?

Sometimes it's easy: a manservant is a servant who happens to be a man; a ferryman is a man who is in charge of a ferry. But not all the words that begin or end with those three letters have anything to do with men. Try your luck with these.

Caiman a) A priest b) A reptile c) A spice

Dragoman a) A guide b) A horse-drawn cart c) A sea monster

Manatee a) A charm or spell b) A monkey c) A sea mammal

Mandala a) An anteater b) A symbol c) A vegetable

Mandate a) A commission b) A handicap c) A secret meeting

Mandible a) A bone b) A medieval ship c) A musical instrument

Mandolin a) A fruit b) A monkey c) A musical instrument

Mandrake a) A bird b) A monkey c) A poisonous plant

Mangosteen a) A drinking glass b) A precious stone c) A tropical fruit

Manifest a) Deceptive b) Obvious c) Troublesome

Manifold a) Having many different kinds b) A political commitment c) A strong paper used for wrapping

Manipulate a) To handle b) To predict c) To send

Manna a) An African antelope b) A tropical fruit c) An unexpected gift

Mansard a) A difficult task b) An encyclopedia c) A roof

Mantilla a) A head-covering b) A monkey c) A predatory insect

Mantra a) A head-covering b) A sacred word c) An African tree

Manzanilla a) An orchard fruit b) A sherry c) A shrub

Ottoman a) An officer b) A seat c) A tropical fruit

Shaman a) A pretence b) A priest c) A punishment

Talisman a) A domestic servant b) A good-luck charm c) A sofa

Answers

Caiman b) A reptile, a tropical relation of the crocodile and alligator. Also spelled *cayman*.

Dragoman a) A guide or interpreter in the Middle East, historically someone who was hired to take intrepid (and probably eccentric) European travellers into unknown territory.

Manatee c) A sea mammal, the size of a small whale, found in tropical waters.

Mandala b) A symbol of the universe in Hinduism and Buddhism. Usually in the form of a circle.

Mandate a) A commission, particularly the authority given to a government by virtue of the electorate having voted it into office: *the party had a mandate to introduce sweeping tax reforms.*

Mandible a) A bone – the lower jawbone in vertebrates. Also, the (non-bony) mouthparts in insects used for biting and crushing food.

Mandolin c) A musical instrument with four strings, related to the lute.

Mandrake c) A poisonous plant, reputed to scream if you pull it up by the roots. Also said to have magic powers and likely to be familiar to anyone who has studied Herbology at Hogwarts.

Mangosteen c) A tropical fruit from Southeast Asia. Nothing like a mango, this is a sweet fleshy fruit enclosed in a hard case.

Manifest b) Obvious, easily noticed: a voluptuously shaped woman might be described as having *manifest charms.* Also a verb: a ghost may sometimes *manifest* itself – appear in visible form where previously it's just made scary noises. A political *manifesto*, a statement of a party's plans and policies, comes originally from the same Latin root.

Manifold a) Having many different kinds – *many fold*, as opposed to only *twofold* or *threefold*: *they gave us manifold excuses for the train being delayed, but I'd have preferred a refund.*

Manipulate a) To handle, usually with skill and sometimes for dishonest purposes. You can, if you are clever enough, *manipulate a screwdriver* into a tight corner, *manipulate the accounts* so that you pay less tax or *manipulate a person* to make them do what you want.

Manna c) An unexpected gift, often *manna from heaven* – a reference to the Old Testament story of the Children of Israel being miraculously fed in the desert, with a bread that they called *manna*: it was white like coriander seed and tasted like wafers made with honey. Nowadays, *manna* can be anything welcome: rain after a drought could be *manna to the garden*, while a politician with wild hair or a long nose is *manna to the cartoonists*.

Mansard c) A roof with two sloping sections on each side, the lower being steeper than the upper. It's a French word, taken from the name of the architect who popularized the style in the seventeenth century, and can also apply to the attic formed by such a roof.

Mantilla a) A head-covering like a scarf or shawl, made of lace or silk and often worn – originally in Spain – over a tall comb in the hair. A Spanish word meaning 'little cloak'.

Mantra b) A sacred word or syllable in Hinduism and Buddhism, of which the most famous is *Om*, repeated to aid concentration during meditation. From the Sanskrit for 'instrument of thought', it's now often used to mean nothing more spiritual than a slogan or catchphrase: *The customer is always right; that's our mantra.*

Manzanilla b) A Spanish sherry, pale and dry. In Spanish *manzanilla* means chamomile, but it also means 'small apple'; the sherry is so called either because its scent is reminiscent of chamomile or because it is made from grapes that resemble small apples. Opinions differ.

Ottoman b) A seat or footstool, padded, upholstered and often hinged so that it also acts as a storage chest. Named after the fabric that originally covered it (*velours ottoman* or Ottoman velvet), which in turn takes its name from the dynasty that ruled Turkey and a substantial empire from the thirteenth to the early twentieth centuries.

Shaman b) A priest or medicine man in certain religions of northern Asia, North America and elsewhere that centre round good and evil spirits that only the shaman can control.

Talisman b) A good-luck charm, specifically one that is supposed to ward off evil spirits or bad things generally. A word of complicated origin that can be traced back to the Greek for a ritual.

I don't want to complain ...

Sticking with the biblical theme (see *A Slip of the Tongue*, page 78), a *jeremiad* is a long, mournful complaint. It derives from the Old Testament prophet *Jeremiah* who, in addition to having a book under his own name, is traditionally credited with writing the one called Lamentations. Jeremiah was persecuted by all sorts of people from his own relatives to the invading Babylonians and had quite a lot to complain about. However justified his complaints may have been, though, the implication of a *jeremiad* is that it goes on a bit.

Words from French

---~~---

The Norman Conquest of 1066 brought Norman French – the language of the conquerors – to Britain, adding reams of vocabulary to the existing Anglo-Saxon tongue. For several centuries French was the language of the court and the aristocracy. Then the seventeenth- and eighteenth-century habit of sending wealthy young men on a 'Grand Tour' of the Continent meant that any educated person spoke both French and Italian, and sprinkling your conversation with French words became a sophisticated thing to do. See how many you recognize.

Bijou a) Dismissive of new ideas b) Having two cheeks c) Small and elegant

Blasé a) Burned b) Deafened c) Indifferent

Bourgeois a) Conventional b) Impatient c) Neglectful

Chic a) Chirpy b) Elegant c) Leisurely

Connoisseur a) An expert b) A know-all c) A professor

Debacle a) A beginning b) A disaster c) A riot

Dénouement a) An assault b) An outcome c) A storehouse

Doyen a) A generous donor or supporter b) A merchant c) A senior person

Ennui a) Boredom b) Effort c) Separation

Gauche a) Clumsy b) Flashy c) Greedy

Louche a) Disreputable b) Flea-ridden c) Relaxed

Nonchalant a) Non-existent b) Obscure c) Unconcerned

Oeuvre a) An eye disease b) An opening c) Work

Panache a) A cure-all b) An overview c) A sense of style

Passé a) Affectionate b) Out of date c) Peaceful

Protégé a) A cabinet or strong box b) A protester c) A pupil

Raconteur a) A hunter b) A rabble-rousing orator c) A storyteller

Rapport a) An emotional bond b) A report c) A scolding

Renaissance a) Denial b) Rebirth c) Reining in, controlling

Sangfroid a) Calmness b) Coldness c) Radiance

Answers

Bijou c) Small and elegant. The normal French word for a jewel, it's often used sarcastically in English: *a bijou residence* is rather self-conscious in its neatness, a bit twee.

Blasé c) Indifferent; unable to enjoy something pleasurable because you've been exposed to it too often: *after ten years in a fifteenth-storey office, she was completely blasé about the glorious view.* You can also be blasé about something unpleasant or dangerous: *he had become blasé about the perils of driving in Naples, which had terrified him when he first moved there.*

Bourgeois a) Conventional. Used to described a stereotypical member of the middle class, with unimaginative, materialistic values and an overdeveloped concern for what the neighbours will think. From the word for a citizen.

Chic b) Elegant, fashionable, stylish. *Chic* can also be a noun, meaning style and elegance, particularly the effortless elegance so envied by those of us who don't have it.

Connoisseur a) An expert, one with specialist knowledge – especially of food, wine or the arts. From the verb *connaître*, meaning to know.

Debacle b) A disaster, a complete failure or collapse. Can be pronounced to rhyme with *the tackle*, or in the French way, more like *day-bark-le*.

Dénouement b) An outcome. From the French for untying a knot, this is the unravelling of a plot at the end of a play, film and so on; more generally, it's what happens at the end of a quarrel or a crisis.

Doyen c) A senior person, a respected member of a profession – the *doyen* (or female *doyenne*) – *of theatrical directors*, say, or *of the diplomatic corps*.

Ennui a) Boredom, particularly the kind that makes you feel languid and dismal – perhaps because you have become too *blasé* (see above) to enjoy yourself.

Gauche a) Clumsy. *Gauche* is the French for left and the suggestion is that left-handed people are either physically clumsy or socially tactless and awkward, or both. This is in painful contrast to the right-handed majority, who are by definition *adroit* – skilful, adept, from *droit*, meaning right. It's worth noting, in passing, that the Latin for left is *sinister* and for right, *dexter*, from which we derive *dextrous*. So this prejudice against the left and the left-handed goes back a long way.

Louche a) Disreputable, shady, shifty – not someone from whom you would buy a used car. The verb *loucher* means to squint, so a louche person literally can't – or won't – look you in the eye.

Nonchalant c) Unconcerned. The middle of the word comes from *chaleur*, meaning warmth, so to be nonchalant is to be cool, chilled, relaxed about the outcome of the matter in hand.

Oeuvre c) Work, particularly the output of an author, composer or other artist. An *hors d'oeuvre* is literally 'outside the work', not served as part of the main meal.

Panache c) A sense of style, a swaggering, theatrical way of going about things, quite different from the quiet elegance of *chic* (see above). A cure-all is a *panacea* and an overview is a *panorama*.

Passé b) Out of date, from the word for *past*. To be *passé* is to be past one's prime, out of fashion, *so* last year.

Protégé c) A pupil. Literally, someone who is protected – usually someone who has been taken under the wing of a senior person and promoted or given opportunities they might not otherwise have had.

Raconteur c) A storyteller, someone with a store of anecdotes who relates them well.

Rapport a) An emotional bond between two or more people. The French word originally meant either a relationship (of any kind, good, bad or indifferent) or the sort of report you might bring home from school or that a police officer might make on an incident. In English, that second sense is generally rendered by *report*; the relationship described by *rapport* is cordial and suggests a special, underlying sympathy and understanding.

Renaissance b) Rebirth or revival, usually of culture or learning. The Renaissance, with a capital R, refers to a specific period of European history in which there was a huge growth in the arts, science and philosophical thought (and a *rebirth* of interest in Classical Greece and Rome – hence the name). Usually considered to have begun in Italy in the fourteenth century, the Renaissance spread across Europe and embraced the work of the painters and sculptors Michelangelo, Jan van Eyck and Hieronymus Bosch; the philosophers Erasmus, Calvin and Thomas More; writers such as William Shakespeare, François Rabelais and Michel de Montaigne; and Leonardo da Vinci, whose many talents included art, science, architecture, anatomy, writing, music and engineering. Few of us would lay claim to a CV like Leonardo's, but today, the term *Renaissance man* (or *woman*) means one who has broad interests in a number of fields.

Sangfroid a) Calmness. The French literally means 'cold blood' but in English to have sangfroid is not the same as being cold-blooded. It means being composed, carrying something off with style. It's more stylish than *nonchalance* (see above), which has a sense of simply not caring. If you have sangfroid, you may still care – it's just that you can deal with a situation in which others might panic.

Words from other European languages

~

French is probably our richest source of borrowings (see page 84), but we've taken our share from the rest of Europe too. In addition to choosing the meanings, see if you know which language these come from.

Aficionado a) An enthusiast b) A love letter c) A story

Brio a) A draught b) Liveliness c) A style of painting

Cognoscenti a) Deep thought b) The pieces of a puzzle c) Those in the know

Diktat a) A decree b) A medicine c) A 'set text' for an exam

Doppelgänger a) A beer b) A lookalike c) A workman

Ersatz a) Artificial b) Obsolete c) Ugly

Gauntlet a) A bay or inlet b) A punishment c) A snack

Hinterland a) A outlying area b) A poor neighbourhood c) A source of wealth

Hubris a) Arrogance b) Hesitation c) Rage

Incognito a) Illiterate b) In disguise c) Thoughtless

Incommunicado a) Helpless b) Isolated c) Sulky

Junta a) A celebration b) A crossroads c) A group in power

Kaput a) Heavy b) Ignorant c) Ruined

Kitsch a) Cheap and tasteless b) Overcooked c) Unlucky

Maelstrom a) Confusion b) Physical strength c) Terror

Mazurka a) A dance b) A head-covering c) A tree

Ombudsman a) An authority b) An independent judge c) A junior musician

Peccadillo a) Pickled vegetables b) A pig c) A small fault

Poltergeist a) A coward b) A mineral c) A spirit

Spiel a) A mirror b) Plausible talk c) A spillage or mess

Zeitgeist a) The attitudes of a certain time b) An elegantly dressed man c) A ghost

---

CONFUSABLES

definite/definitive

Definite means 'clearly defined, exact'; *definitive* is 'providing the final, unarguable answer'. A doctor's *definite opinion*, however firmly expressed, could be wrong; a *definitive diagnosis* removes any doubt about what the problem is.

Answers

Aficionado a) An enthusiast, particularly a sports fan: *a tennis aficionado*. From the Spanish for passion.

Brio b) Liveliness – an Italian word often used in music: many works contain the instruction to play *con brio*.

Cognoscenti c) Those in the know, particularly those who are well informed about one of the arts: *the cognoscenti go to end-of-year shows in the hope of discovering a promising artist before anyone else does*. From the Italian. Deep thought is *cogitation*.

Diktat a) A decree, a severe decision imposed on a defeated nation by a victorious one. A German word related to *dictator* and, more loosely, to *dictum* (see page 67).

Doppelgänger b) A lookalike, literally (from German) a 'double goer', someone who looks exactly like you and, according to tradition, walks by your side and brings bad luck. Not quite the same as an *alter ego* (Latin for 'other self'), which is a different personality living in your body, Jekyll-and-Hyde style. In looser use, an *alter ego* can be a close friend who looks nothing like you; a *doppelgänger* bears a strong physical resemblance though you may never have met them, let alone become bosom buddies.

Ersatz a) Artificial, a cheap imitation of the real thing. If you broke into the Louvre and swapped *an ersatz Mona Lisa* for the original, no one would be fooled for a moment. From the German for substitute.

Gauntlet b) A punishment, as in *running the gauntlet* – from a Swedish military discipline in which the person being punished ran between two lines of men who beat him with sticks or knotted rope. Nowadays used in the figurative sense of enduring an ordeal: *I have to run the gauntlet of the examining body if I want to do a doctorate*. In the seventeenth century, the punishment was called *gantlope*, which is more like the original

Swedish. But the English also had *gauntlets*, the heavy armoured gloves worn in medieval battles or their lighter and later equivalent, used to strike someone on the cheek if you were challenging them to a duel. That word derives from French, but you can see how people managed to muddle the two together.

Hinterland a) An outlying area, from the German for 'beyond'. Evelyn Waugh, in his novel *Brideshead Revisited*, describes a group of soldiers getting off a tram and proceeding on foot to their new camp: *This was the extreme limit of the city. Here the close, homogeneous territory of housing estates and cinemas ended and the hinterland began.* It conjures up perfectly the vague bleakness of the word.

Hubris a) Arrogance, the sort of pride that comes before a fall. From Greek, and used with reference to Classical drama to describe the tragic flaw in the hero's character that led to his undoing.

Incognito b) In disguise, under an assumed name and probably wearing dark glasses: the way a famous person or spy travels if he doesn't want to be recognized (if such a person is female, she is *incognita*). From the Italian for unknown.

Incommunicado b) Isolated, literally (in Spanish) 'deprived of communication'. In English it could mean that you were in solitary confinement, or merely that you were in a meeting and weren't to be disturbed.

Junta c) A group in power, particularly a small group that has come to power after a coup. From Spanish.

Kaput c) Ruined, broken, used particularly of something that has broken down because it is old or has outlived its usefulness – anything from an IT system to a political one. From German.

Kitsch a) Cheap and tasteless, again from German. Gift shops are often accused of selling *kitsch souvenirs* (or just *kitsch*) – mementos of a royal wedding, perhaps, or super-cute little stuffed animals. Such items are often very popular, so describing them as *kitsch* lets everyone know that you have more sophisticated taste.

Words from other European languages

Maelstrom a) Confusion, the sort caused by a mass of objects spinning about: *a maelstrom of reporters forced their way into the courtroom to hear the verdict.* From the name of a whirlpool near the Lofoten Islands in Norway, said to suck passing vessels into it and destroy them, and also applied to any other powerful whirlpool. The first syllable is pronounced *mail*.

Mazurka a) A lively dance, originating in Poland and named after the province of Mazur or Mazovia. The New Zealand tree, from which expensive honey is made, is the *manuka*.

Ombudsman b) An independent judge appointed to arbitrate on matters where the two parties (management and trades union, for example) have failed to reach agreement. From a Swedish word for commissioner, because it was the Swedish Parliament that first used such a system.

Peccadillo c) A small fault, Spanish for 'little sin': *chocolate is only a peccadillo, after all, not really a vice.* Pickled vegetables are *piccalilli* and there is a South American pig called a *peccary*.

Poltergeist c) A spirit, the sort of ghost that makes itself unpopular by breaking the crockery and moving the furniture around. From the German for 'noisy spirit'; see *zeitgeist*, below.

Spiel b) Plausible talk that has no substance to it, such as the patter salespeople come out with in an effort to persuade you to buy their wares. A German word, pronounced to rhyme with *peel*. The German term for mirror is *Spiegel*, as in *Der Spiegel*, the weekly news magazine.

Zeitgeist a) The attitudes of a certain time. A rather pretentious word, used particularly in critiques of a film or literary work: *with its Bowie soundtrack and passion for flared trousers, it really captured the 1970s zeitgeist.* German for 'time spirit'.

Over and under

Words beginning with *sub-* usually mean something to do with 'under'; *super-* is 'over' or 'above'. How many of these do you know?

Subaltern a) Confusing b) A junior officer c) Neither one thing nor the other, moderate

Subcutaneous a) Fussy b) Past one's best c) Under the skin

Subjective a) Bossy b) Personal c) Single-minded

Subjugate a) To decide between two options b) To force (someone) to submit c) To list in alphabetical order

Subjunctive a) Expressing doubt b) Obedient c) Paying a regular fee

Subliminal a) Fewer than the number required b) Resulting from processes of which you are unaware c) Underground

Subordinate a) Later b) Less important c) Random, out of order

Subsistence a) Dullness b) Managing to live c) Stubbornness

Substantiate a) To establish as real b) To protect c) To smother

Subsume a) To eat b) To incorporate c) To sink

Subversive a) Corrupting b) Punishing c) Wobbly

Superannuated a) Of excellent quality b) Old c) Thoughtless

Supercilious a) Arrogant b) Flexible c) Tall

Superimpose a) To be taller than b) To put on top of
c) To threaten

Superlative a) Excellent b) Expensive c) Extravagant

Supernova a) An actress b) A spirit in Roman mythology c) A star

Supernumerary a) Extra b) Lazy c) Very enjoyable

Superscript a) Crossed out b) Erect c) Written above the line

Supersede a) To be taller than b) To outrank c) To take the
place of

Supervisory a) Coming after b) Overseeing c) Unnecessary

Answers

Subaltern b) A junior officer – in some armies, a commissioned officer below the rank of captain. Literally 'below the other'.

Subcutaneous c) Under the skin, particularly *a subcutaneous injection*, one that is given below the skin, or *subcutaneous parasites*, but you probably feel itchy just thinking about them.

Subjective b) Personal, as opposed to *objective*, which means based on facts rather than individual opinion or bias: *I think Byron is overrated, but it's a purely subjective view – a lot of people think he's wonderful.*

Subjugate b) To force (someone) to submit: *the new teacher subjugated the class to his authority.* Literally 'under the yoke'.

Subjunctive a) Expressing doubt. A grammatical term denoting the mood of a verb when what is being expressed is uncertain. *If I go now, I'll be there by six o'clock* is a definite statement in what is known as the *indicative* mood; introduce some doubt and you get *if I went now* [which I might not do], *I would be there by six o'clock.* In that sentence, *went* is in the subjunctive. A regular fee – to enable you to belong to a club, for example, or to receive copies of a magazine – is a *subscription*.

Subliminal b) Resulting from processes of which you are unaware. In *subliminal advertising*, promotional images or slogans appear on a film or television screen so briefly that you don't consciously notice them but still absorb the message. (It's illegal in many countries, so don't try it.) Literally 'under the threshold'.

Subordinate b) Less important, under the authority of another: *the officer was always very concerned with the welfare of his subordinates.* The opposite, *insubordinate*, means not recognizing that authority: *the junior officers were reprimanded for insubordination when they refused to salute the general.*

Subsistence b) Managing to live, but without much left over. *Subsistence farmers* consume most of their own produce, with little left to sell; *a subsistence wage* enables you to survive but not to buy designer clothes or take expensive holidays.

Substantiate a) To establish as real: *the eyewitness's evidence substantiated my story*. Literally 'to stand under, to support'.

Subsume b) To incorporate, to take a smaller thing into a larger one: *over the years, the outlying villages were subsumed into the town*. Literally 'to take under'.

Subversive a) Corrupting or undermining something in authority: *subversive humour* pokes fun at 'the establishment'; *subversive activity* might be intended to overthrow a government or a committee. Literally 'to turn from below'.

Superannuated b) Old, out of date, no longer any use. A *superannuated IT system* is in need of replacement or at least a radical overhaul. In Australia, New Zealand and some other countries, the old-age pension is known as *superannuation*. Literally 'above [the required number of] years'.

Supercilious a) Arrogant, looking down on or ignoring someone or something you consider inferior: *she didn't have to tell me I was scruffy – her supercilious look said it all*. From the Latin for eyebrow, a part of the body that really comes into its own when you want to look *supercilious*.

Superimpose b) To put on top of, particularly one image on top of another: *we superimposed my face on to the old photograph, to see what I would have looked like in my grandmother's wedding dress*.

Superlative a) Excellent, of the highest quality: *the winning couple did a superlative rumba*. In grammar, a *superlative* form indicates the most extreme degree of anything, often ending in *-est*: *the prettiest, the loudest* (as opposed to the *comparatives prettier, louder*, which compare only two things). Literally 'carrying above'.

Supernova c) A star, or strictly an event in the life of a star when it explodes to become – for a short while in star terms – incredibly bright in the sky. Literally 'above new', because it is brighter than (or above or better than) a *nova*, another brief but less spectacular starry event.

Supernumerary a) Extra, exceeding the required number: *he functioned as a supernumerary lecturer, helping out when the senior staff needed time off to catch up on their research. Supernumerary* can also be a noun, so that same lecturer could be described as *a supernumerary in the department.*

Superscript c) Written above the line, as in the number two of πr^2. In old-fashioned (pre-digital) correspondence, a *superscription* was either the sender's name and address at the top of a letter or the receiver's details on the outside.

Supersede c) To take the place of, particularly if something has become obsolete or low-tech: *OS X Yosemite superseded earlier software named after big cats.* Literally 'to sit over', and note the *s* (not *c*) in the middle – *supersede* is related to *sedentary, sedate* and other words to do with sitting.

Supervisory b) Overseeing, as in *a supervisory position* – one in which you keep an eye on other people rather than doing the work yourself.

⟨ CONFUSABLES ⟩

alternate/alternative

To *alternate* is to occur by turns – *night alternates with day* – or to interchange between two things – *he alternates between being an actor by night and a barista by day.* That hard-working person might get *alternate Sundays* off – he works one Sunday but not the next. An *alternative* is an option, a choice (strictly speaking between only two things): *we'll have to walk – the bus has been cancelled, so we have no alternative.*

Are you with me or against me?

Words beginning *con-* or *com-* often mean something to do with 'with'; *contra-* is likely to mean 'against'. How many of these can you sort out?

Combustion a) Burning b) Explosion c) Feasting

Compendium a) A collection b) Peacefulness c) Understanding

Complacent a) Being an accomplice b) Eager to please c) Pleased with oneself

Complementary a) Going together b) Polite c) Praising

Conciliate a) To discuss b) To make legal c) To make peace with

Confederate a) A director b) A member of Parliament c) A partner in crime

Conglomerate a) Confusion b) A group of companies c) An incorrect conclusion

Congruous a) Agreeing b) Being in a sexual relationship c) Bewildered

Conjecture a) A guess b) A medical treatment c) A society

Connive a) To enclose b) To prove c) To scheme

Consternation a) Dismay b) A fire c) A riot

Contextualize a) To learn by heart b) To please c) To set in relevant circumstances

Contraband a) A form of birth control b) A one-way system c) Smuggled goods

Contradictory a) Inconsistent b) Shortening c) Unsafe

Contrapuntal a) Argumentative b) Inconsistent c) To do with two melodies being played together

Contravene a) To arrive late b) To break a rule c) To deny

Contretemps a) An awkward situation b) Bad weather c) A disappointing outcome or let-down

Contusion a) An awkward situation b) A bruise c) A disturbance

Convivial a) Complicated b) Following accepted usage c) Sociable

Convoluted a) Complicated b) Sociable c) Well-informed

Answers

Combustion a) Burning – a term usually used in chemistry and with reference to the *internal combustion engine* of a vehicle.

Compendium a) A collection, as in a book containing a compilation of facts or hints (*a compendium of knitting techniques*), or *a compendium of games* – a number of games packaged together and sold as a single item.

Complacent c) Pleased with oneself – not a compliment, and not to be confused with *complaisant*, which means easy-going, eager to please others.

Complementary a) Going together to make a whole, as in *complementary colours* – two colours that in the correct proportion combine to make black or white – or *complementary medicine*, which acts alongside conventional medicine. Praising, as in paying someone a *compliment*, is *complimentary*.

Conciliate c) To make peace with, to stop someone from being angry (or an enemy from being hostile) by making friendly or soothing approaches. You might go into a potentially difficult meeting with the intention of *conciliating* the various factions, rather than taking a confrontational approach.

Confederate c) A partner in crime, someone who joins you in a conspiracy. A *confederation* (or in US history a *Confederacy*, the southern states in the Civil War) is not necessarily a bad thing – it may simply be a union of states or other political bodies, as in the *Swiss Confederation*, the official name for Switzerland. But when you describe an individual as a *confederate*, it's likely that you are both up to no good.

Conglomerate b) A group of companies joined under the same management but dealing in a wide range of goods and services.

Congruous a) Agreeing. *Congruence* is a complicated concept in maths to do with the relationship between two integers, but *congruous* can be used more generally to describe things that fit together or are appropriate. Its opposite, *incongruous*, is more common: *he looked quite incongruous in the photo, wearing a suit when everyone else was dressed for sunbathing.*

Conjecture a) A guess, a conclusion based on incomplete evidence: *I haven't the slightest conjecture where they are; I haven't heard from them for a month.*

Connive c) To scheme, to plot with someone to achieve an immoral or illegal end: *the CEO refused to resign, so the directors had to find a way to connive at his downfall.*

Consternation a) Dismay, coupled with anxiety, confusion and possibly guilt at being taken by surprise: *when the police arrived, he looked around in consternation, wondering if he could climb out the window on to the roof.* A serious fire is a *conflagration.*

Contextualize c) To set in relevant circumstances, to consider (a historical event, perhaps, or a piece of literature) in its *context.*

Contraband c) Smuggled goods. A word of complicated origin that came into English from Spanish and has nothing to do with *contraception* or birth control. A one-way system (set up on a British motorway when road works are in progress) is a *contraflow.*

Contradictory a) Inconsistent, illogical, as in a statement that *contradicts* or goes against something that has been said previously.

Contrapuntal c) To do with two melodies being played together, in *counterpoint* – for example, when a descant is played or sung at a higher pitch than the main theme. *Counterpoint* may also be used in a non-musical sense to mean a foil, something that makes one thing stand out against another.

Contravene b) To break a rule, usually in a formal sense: *the invasion contravened the treaty that had been signed the previous year.*

Contretemps a) An awkward situation, an embarrassing disagreement (originally a mistimed piece of swordplay in fencing). It comes from the French for 'against the time', suggesting that it is the timing of the disagreement, rather than its substance, that is embarrassing: *we were in the middle of a domestic contretemps when the first guests arrived.*

Contusion b) A bruise, from the Latin for to beat.

Convivial c) Sociable, from the Latin for living together. A *convivial person* is happy in the company of others; a *convivial evening* involves cheerful conversation and probably a certain amount of alcohol. Following accepted usage is *conventional*; for *complicated*, see the next entry.

Convoluted a) Complicated, hard to follow, as in a *convoluted literary style* or a *convoluted argument*. It's from the Latin for turning or coiling and related to the plant *Convolvulus*, known for its twisting tendrils. Well-informed is *conversant*.

Body language

You're probably familiar with *flatulence* or *flatus* as more elegant terms for another word beginning with *f* and meaning breaking wind. We can disguise the body's other embarrassing noises under technical terms, too.

- **Eructation** – better known as burping, from the Latin for to emit.
- **Singultus** – from the Latin for a sob or speech broken by sobs (who knew there was a word for that?). Lord Byron used it in this sense; a doctor would mean hiccups.

And best of all:

- **Borborygmus**, rumbling in the tummy. An Ancient Greek word, suggesting that even the Mediterranean diet didn't leave you immune. If you're wondering how to work this into a conversation, the *Oxford English Dictionary* cites this useful quotation from H. G. Wells, writing in the *Sunday Express* newspaper in 1927: *Elephant hunters say that they can tell the proximity of a herd by the borborygmic noises the poor brutes emit.*

One or many?

———————~———————

Here's another section where the start of the word will help you: *mono-* means 'one' and *poly-* means 'many'. Can you decipher the rest?

Monochrome a) In black and white b) Having a shiny metallic surface c) Wandering

Monocycle a) An eyeglass b) A one-wheeled vehicle c) A short life

Monograph a) A design based on initials b) An essay on a specific subject c) A wireless communication system

Monolith a) An exercise programme b) A form of printing c) A large block of stone

Monologue a) A simple meal b) A straightforward argument c) An uninterrupted speech

Monomania a) Being faithful to your partner b) Having good manners c) An obsession

Monophagy a) Able to live only in a specific environment b) Eating only one type of food c) Living for only one year

Monopoly a) Exclusive control b) One of many c) Speaking only one language

Monosyllabic a) Abrupt b) Offering no choice c) In poetry, having short lines

One or many?

Monotheistic a) Having one god b) Sticking closely to one subject c) Tuneless

Monotonous a) Boring b) Heavy c) Quick-witted

Polygamous a) Having many fingers b) Having many spouses c) Having many talents

Polyglot a) Greedy b) Speaking many languages c) Sticky

Polygon a) A complicated family tree b) A many-sided figure c) A painting with many panels

Polygraph a) A letter written with the lines crossed over each other at right angles to avoid having to use a second sheet of paper b) A lie detector c) A thesis

Polymath a) An abacus b) A person with wide-ranging interests c) An animal that takes different forms in the course of its life

Polymer a) A compound made up of many repeated units b) A person with wide-ranging interests c) A solid figure with four or more faces

Polyp a) A blip on a computer screen b) A growth c) A stretch of open water

Polypody a) A centipede b) A tropical climbing plant c) A type of fern

Polystyrene a) An artificial sweetener b) A figure of speech used in rhetoric c) A synthetic material

Polyunsaturate a) A type of chromosome b) A type of fat c) A type of plastic

Answers

Monochrome a) In black and white. Strictly speaking monochrome means 'one colour', and the term can be employed for an artwork using different tones of the same colour, but it is more often used with reference to a black-and-white photograph or film.

Monocycle b) A one-wheeled vehicle, often also referred to as a unicycle (*uni* comes from the Latin for one; *mono* is the Greek equivalent). An eyeglass designed to fit one eye, as opposed to a pair of spectacles designed for both eyes, is a *monocle*.

Monograph b) An essay on a specific subject. In the short story 'The Boscombe Valley Mystery' Sherlock Holmes refers to a monograph he has written on the difference among ashes of 140 varieties of tobacco; in 'A Case of Identity' he mentions plans for another on the typewriter's relation to crime. A design based on initials, such as might be embroidered on a tie or handkerchief, is a *monogram*.

Monolith c) A large block of stone or a statue cut from a single block of stone. The word can also be used metaphorically: a *monolithic* person is intractable, not easy to persuade. The form of printing is *lithography*.

Monologue c) An uninterrupted speech by one person. This can be on the stage, particularly when the character is alone – a stand-up comedian's routine could be described as a monologue, until he or she starts interacting with the audience. Or it can be in conversation, when a single person is dominating, usually in a boring way.

Monomania c) An obsession – having a mania for one thing to the exclusion of all else, such as Captain Ahab pursuing the whale in Herman Melville's novel *Moby-Dick*.

Monophagy b) Eating only one type of food. Insects in particular can be very fussy when it comes to diet, and whole populations can be wiped out if their favourite crop fails.

One or many?

Monopoly a) Exclusive control of the supply of goods or services in a given market. The point of the game Monopoly is to acquire so much property that you drive your opponents into bankruptcy; in real life it is much the same.

Monosyllabic a) Abrupt, saying very little, as in the answers to 'How was school?' 'Fine.' 'Did you get your essay back?' 'Yes.' 'What sort of mark did you get?' 'Fine.' Any parent of a teenager will recognize this at a glance.

Monotheistic a) Having one god. Christianity, Judaism and Islam are *monotheistic* religions; Hinduism, to name but one, is *polytheistic*, having lots of gods.

Monotonous a) Boring. A sequence of *monotones* in speech or sound has no variety – it's all at the same level, with no ups or downs, so becomes dull after a (very short) while.

Polygamous b) Having many spouses, as opposed to *monogamous* (having one spouse) or *bigamous* (having two). A creature with many fingers is *polydactylous*.

Polyglot b) Speaking many languages. The Latin-derived word *multilingual* means the same thing.

Polygon b) A many-sided figure, a term from geometry that embraces all sorts of two-dimensional figures with three or more straight sides. Polygons with three and four sides are *triangles* and *quadrilaterals* respectively; those with more sides use the Greek prefixes of number (a *pentagon* has five sides, a *hexagon* six and so on). A painting with many panels is a *polyptych*.

Polygraph b) A lie detector, an instrument that – according to the derivation of the word – 'writes copiously', detecting changes in blood pressure, perspiration and the like that might indicate that the person being tested is lying.

Polymath b) A person with wide-ranging interests. The *math* part comes from the Greek for a science, and reappears in *mathematics* (literally 'concerned with learning in general' rather than with sums in particular).

Polymer a) A compound made up of many repeated units, such as starch or Perspex. The solid figure is a *polyhedron*.

Polyp b) A growth, which may be malignant or benign, that projects from a mucous membrane in various parts of the body. You have to go quite a long way back into this word's origins to find anything meaning 'many', but it does ultimately derive from a Greek word meaning 'many feet' (see next entry).

Polypody c) A type of fern, so called because it has deeply divided leaves that make it look as if it has 'many feet'.

Polystyrene c) A synthetic material, from which we make insulated cups and that rigid white foam used for packing.

Polyunsaturate b) A type of fat, the 'good' kind that is less likely to be converted to cholesterol in the human body.

Words that are hard to spell

Most of us probably know what broccoli and cemetery mean, even if we aren't sure how to spell them. But here are a group of less familiar words that may also present spelling problems. How many of them do you know?

Acquiescent a) Greedy, materialistic b) Interested, having an enquiring mind c) Willing to agree

Aegis a) Enthusiasm b) Protection c) Tenderness

Archetype a) A printing font b) A style of column in Classical architecture c) A typical specimen

Assimilate a) To arrange to meet b) To copy c) To learn and understand

Cerebral Relating to … a) the brain b) the digestion c) the liver

Chimera a) An African antelope b) A chemical reaction c) A dream or fantasy

Desiccate a) To dry out b) To indicate or specify c) To separate

Dystopia a) An eye disease b) A lack of coordination c) An unpleasant place

Excrescence a) A cry of pain b) An excuse c) An outgrowth

Feasible a) Laughable b) Possible c) Practical

Heinous a) Awkward b) Evil c) Unaware

Hieroglyphic Relating to ... a) authority b) picture writing c) priests

Idiosyncrasy a) A bright idea b) A stupid idea c) A type of behaviour

Indict a) To accuse b) To disagree c) To write down

Languor a) A long-tailed monkey b) Weariness c) The wood of a tropical tree

Oscillate a) To bang b) To kiss c) To swing from side to side

Paraphernalia a) Anxiety b) Meanness c) Miscellaneous stuff

Quandary a) A difficult situation b) A government department c) A large quantity

Sacrilege a) Abusing something sacred b) Giving up something valuable c) Inflicting unnecessary pain

Triskaidekaphobia Fear of ... a) cats b) snakes c) the number thirteen

Answers

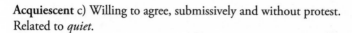

Acquiescent c) Willing to agree, submissively and without protest. Related to *quiet*.

Aegis b) Protection, sponsorship, usually in the expression *under the aegis of*. The original *aegis* was something – possibly a shield – that Greek gods carried in battle, to protect themselves and the mortals they favoured.

Archetype c) A typical or perfect specimen, as in *the archetype of a Hollywood hero* – one who might be played by John Wayne, Bruce Willis or Idris Elba, depending on your taste and generation.

Assimilate c) To learn and understand thoroughly (*she assimilated the information*), to become adjusted to a new situation (*they assimilated quickly into life in the wilderness*). The bit in the middle is indeed related to *similar*.

Cerebral a) Relating to the brain, either literally, as in a *cerebral haemorrhage* or *cerebral palsy*, or figuratively, meaning involving the intelligence and rational thought rather than the emotions.

Chimera c) A wild and unrealistic dream or fantasy. This is another word derived from Greek mythology – the original *chimera* or *chimaera* was a fire-breathing monster with the head of a lion, the body of a goat and the tail of a serpent.

Desiccate a) To dry out, particularly as a way of preserving food (*desiccated coconut*). To indicate or specify is to *designate*.

Dystopia c) An unpleasant place, an imaginary setting, usually in the future, where everything is horrible. The opposite of a *Utopia*. Novels set in such places – George Orwell's *Nineteen Eighty-Four* and Margaret Atwood's *The Handmaid's Tale*, for example – may also be *dystopias* or *dystopian fiction*.

Excrescence c) An outgrowth or protuberance, usually from an organ or on the surface of the body or of a plant, likely to be disfiguring and a sign of disease: *the white excrescences spread from tree to tree and soon killed the whole orchard.* From Latin for 'growing out' and related to *crescendo*.

Feasible b) Possible, able to be put into practice, perhaps after someone has done *a feasibility study.*

Heinous b) Evil, as in *a heinous crime.* From an old French word meaning hate.

Hieroglyphic b) Relating to picture writing, particularly that associated with Ancient Egypt, where images and symbols were used instead of words.

Idiosyncrasy c) A type of behaviour, a slightly odd characteristic of a certain person: *it was one of his idiosyncrasies that he refused to answer the phone unless he was sitting at his desk.* From Greek words meaning 'individual temperament' and not to be confused with *democracy* and other words ending in *-cracy*, which are to do with government.

Indict a) To accuse, particularly to charge someone formally with a crime. Pronounced *indite*.

Languor b) Weariness, either physical or mental – a disinclination to do anything or take an interest in anything. If you display this, you are *languid;* both are related to *languish* and come from a French word for 'to droop in spirits'. *Languishing* conveys not only weariness but also being weak or in a state of hardship: *he languished in prison for ten years.* There is also the sense of *becoming* weak – *he languished for lack of food* – and of pining for something unobtainable – *he languished for love of her.* The long-tailed monkey is a *langur*.

Oscillate c) To swing from side to side, either literally, like the pendulum of a clock, or figuratively, to waver between opinions or courses of action. *Vacillate* is similar, but carries the suggestion that you are hesitating to make up your mind at all. To kiss is to *osculate*.

Paraphernalia c) Miscellaneous stuff, an individual's possessions or the things needed for a particular activity: *I have to take a lot of paraphernalia with me for the weekend because the weather is so unreliable.*

Quandary a) A difficult situation, a dilemma. To be *in a quandary* is to be faced with a tricky decision, in which no answer is likely to be entirely satisfactory.

Sacrilege a) Abusing something sacred or worthy of respect. This can be serious or jokey: *the vandals committed an act of sacrilege when they ransacked the temple* or *she was rude about Pierce Brosnan's singing: what sacrilege!* Giving up something valuable may be a *sacrifice*, while inflicting unnecessary pain – and getting pleasure from it – is *sadism*.

Triskaidekaphobia c) Fear of the number thirteen. Any word ending in *-phobia* refers to an abnormal, unhealthy fear. The fear of cats is *ailurophobia* and of snakes *ophiophobia*.

CONFUSABLES

allay/alley/alloy/ally

You can *allay* a person's fears or suspicions (put them to rest) by showing them there is nothing to worry about in the *alley* (a narrow lane). That person might then become an *ally* (a friend, someone fighting on your side). An *alloy* is a metallic material formed by mixing two or more metals and sometimes other substances – bronze is an *alloy* made from copper and tin; steel is an *alloy* based on iron and carbon.

Here's looking at you, kid

Some terms from the worlds of film and photography – a few technical, a few jargon and a few that might be useful in the wider world.

Bracketing a) Performing your own stunts b) Photographing or filming through a 'frame' such as a doorway c) Taking several shots of the same subject

CGI a) Cinema-going industry b) Computer-generated imagery c) Computer-graphic illustration

Continuity a) Another term for a sequel b) Consistency of detail c) Smooth transition from one scene to another

Cross-over a) Appealing to unexpected audiences b) Mixing live action and special effects c) Mixing silent and 'talkie' sequences

Ensemble a) A costume designer b) A large cast with no obvious starring role c) A rehearsal of crowd scenes

Film noir A film that … a) deals with dark, morally ambiguous themes b) makes reference to earlier films on the same theme c) was shot in black and white after colour had become the norm

Fish-eye a) A low level of light b) Physical comedy, slapstick c) A type of lens

Flashback a) Another term for back-lighting b) A sequence set in an earlier time c) A technique for simulating an explosion

Fourth wall a) A final draft of a script b) The imaginary barrier between audience and action c) An unstable set

Homage a) A close-up, detail shot b) A domestic comedy c) A tribute

Lampoon a) A horror film b) A lighting effect c) A satire

Longueur a) A boring bit b) An epic c) A long shot, as opposed to a close-up

Pan a) A cylinder for holding film b) A large light c) A scanning shot

Pastiche a) A collection of photos combined to make a single image b) An imitation c) Reflected light

Rushes a) The result of a day's filming b) Retouching c) The climax of a Western

Scenario a) A backdrop or flat piece of scenery b) A production assistant c) A summary of the plot

Swashbuckler a) A flamboyant hero b) A small but important role c) A special effect used in fight scenes

Tag line a) The closing line of dialogue b) Part of the opening credits c) A short, catchy description

Time-lapse a) A delay in filming due to bad weather b) A pause in a soundtrack c) A photographic technique

Vamp a) A lighting device b) A seductive female character c) A single shot or frame of film

Answers

Bracketing c) Taking several shots of the same subject with different levels of light to ensure you obtain the effect you want.

CGI b) Computer-generated imagery – using computer technology to produce images or special effects, as with the dinosaurs in *Jurassic Park* and lots of the clever stuff in the Star Wars and Harry Potter series.

Continuity b) Consistency of detail, ensuring, for example, that a character isn't clean-shaven in one shot and bearded immediately afterwards. Important in cinema (where a *continuity supervisor* is employed to keep an eye on such things), because scenes are not usually shot in chronological order.

Cross-over a) Appealing to unexpected audiences, as when a film apparently aimed at children also appeals to adults, or one focusing on a specific cultural group attracts a multi-cultural audience.

Ensemble b) A large cast with no obvious starring role, but with a number of substantial parts, often all played by well-known actors. From the French for *together*.

Film noir a) A film that deals with dark, morally ambiguous themes, particularly gangster- or crime-based films made in the USA in the 1940s and '50s. *Films noirs* tend to be bleak and fatalistic in tone, and rarely have happy endings. The expression is French for *black film*, but, although most of them were shot in black and white, it's the bleak outlook that is the defining feature.

Fish-eye c) A type of lens with a very wide angle. It produces a distorted effect supposedly resembling the way a fish would see the world.

Flashback b) A sequence set in an earlier time, allowing a character to reminisce about past events and how they led up to the present situation. *Flashforwards* are less common, but can be used to show a character imagining events in the future.

Fourth wall b) The imaginary barrier between audience and action, through which we watch what is going on. The wall is said to be 'broken' when an actor delivers an aside direct to the audience.

Homage c) A tribute to the work of an earlier director, performer or writer: *with its black-and-white photography and tricky camera angles, it was a clear homage to Orson Welles*. Outside the world of film and theatre, a *homage* is a public show of respect: *crowds gathered to pay homage to the dead of two world wars*. If you're being arty, you pronounce this as if it were French, with the *h* silent, the accent on the second syllable and the *a* an *aaah* sound; in unpretentious English the vowels are short (*homm'ge*) and the accent is on the first syllable.

Lampoon c) A satire, as in *National Lampoon* magazine and the spin-off films, which satirized everything under the sun in the 1970s and '80s. As the magazine showed, a *lampoon* doesn't have to be in the best of taste, which makes it tempting to believe the unconfirmed theory that the word comes from the French *lampons*, meaning 'let us drink'.

Longueur a) A boring bit. This is the French word for *length*, used in theatrical circles to describe a slow scene when you wish the playwright would just get on with it, but also in a film for those moments when you realize you should have bought popcorn after all.

Pan c) A scanning shot, made by moving the camera to follow a moving object or to survey a wide scene. This creates the effect of a *panorama*, from which this sort of *pan* is abbreviated. It has nothing to do with *panning* a film, meaning giving it a bad review: that's connected with the sort of *pan* you cook in – or perhaps hit people over the head with.

Pastiche b) An imitation, particularly a humorous and affectionate one, drawing on elements of some earlier work. Sergio Leone's 1960s Spaghetti Westerns are often described as *pastiches* of earlier, traditional Westerns, and were later themselves pastiched in Quentin Tarantino's *Django Unchained*. The stricter, original meaning is a work (of art, literature or music as well as film) that mixes elements from different styles or periods: this is also a *pasticcio*, from the Italian for a pie or pasty made from a variety of ingredients. *Pastiche* is pronounced as if it were French – the *a* is short, as in *pat*, and the last syllable is -*eesh*. A collection of photos combined to make a single image is a *montage*.

Rushes a) The result of a day's filming. Also called the *dailies*, this is the footage that the director and others watch before moving on to the next day's work, to check that they are happy with what they've done. The crime writer Mary Roberts Rinehart used the term as early as 1920, with no suggestion that it was a new coinage, so it must have turned up in Hollywood almost as soon as film and cameras did. It's related to the *rush* that means hurrying, presumably because you rushed through them without any editing.

Scenario c) A summary of the plot, sometimes extended to mean a scene-by-scene breakdown that details what scenery and props are required, which characters are involved and so on. The word is much used outside of the cinema to mean a sequence of events, a set of circumstances, most commonly *worst-case scenario* (frequently abbreviated to *worst case*) – the worst that could possibly happen.

Swashbuckler a) A flamboyant hero or the sort of film or play in which he appears. He (and it generally was a he) wore period costume, brandished a sword (there's nothing swashbuckling about guns), leapt across rooftops or battlements, was charming throughout and always won. Dating back to the sixteenth century, the word is a combination of *swash*, the sound of a sword hitting something, and *buckler*, a shield – so, the sound your sword makes when you strike an opponent's shield. A small but important role played by a famous actor is a *cameo*.

Tag line c) A short, catchy description, a soundbite intended to attract a potential audience. *Just when you thought it was safe to go back in the water* (from *Jaws 2*) and *In space no one can hear you scream* (*Alien*) remain two of the best, though *A little bear will make a big splash* (*Paddington*) shows that they don't all come from 1970s horror films.

Time-lapse c) A photographic technique in which each frame of a film is captured much more slowly than usual, so that when the film is played at normal speed everything appears to be happening very quickly. It can show plants growing, for example, and possibly even paint drying.

Vamp b) A seductive female character, often seen in *films noirs* (see above). Also called a *femme fatale* or 'fatal woman', she generally leads men astray and sometimes causes them to be killed, but although *vamp* is short for *vampire*, she doesn't literally drink blood.

Art for art's sake

Some words from art, literature and theatre – all useful for making you sound cultivated, whether you are or not.

Allegory a) An omnibus edition b) A poem of praise c) A symbolic work

Anthology a) A collection b) Poetic metre c) The study of hymns

Bas-relief a) Close to the audience, down stage b) A form of sculpture c) A painting of a nude

Bravura a) A brilliant passage or performance b) Heavy makeup c) Loud singing

Chiaroscuro a) Abstract b) An arrangement of light and dark c) A transparent curtain

Collage a) A flimsy costume b) Miscellaneous bits pasted together c) A series of works on the same theme

Genre a) A category b) Censorship c) A dramatic monologue

Gouache a) Farce b) Opaque paint c) A type of sculpture

Incunabula a) Early books b) A gig, a one-night engagement c) A young innocent female character

Ingénue a) A one-act play b) A portrait of a child c) A young innocent female character

Juvenilia a) A Latin tragedy b) Works belonging to the author's youth c) A young innocent female character

Kabuki a) Indian dance b) Japanese theatre c) South American sculpture

Novella a) A revival b) A short novel c) A work in nine parts

Palimpsest a) A marble statue b) A reading of a play, without costumes or action c) A recycled manuscript

Pietà a) A depiction of the dead Christ b) A hymn c) A tragic ending, a tear-jerker

Pseudonym a) A false name b) A forgery c) An obscure work

Repertoire a) All the works a company can perform b) A rehearsal c) 'Series paintings', different studies of the same subject

Scansion a) The analysis of the metrical structure of verse
b) A comparative study of different versions of a text
c) A read-through of a play

Thespian a) An actor b) A musician c) A sculptor

Triptych a) A farce b) A portrait of Christ c) A set of three connected paintings

Answers

Allegory c) A symbolic work of art or literature in which the surface meaning is used to convey a deeper moral message. John Bunyan's seventeenth-century Christian allegory *A Pilgrim's Progress*, for example, contains characters called Giant Despair (who lives in Doubting Castle), Obstinate, Pliable and Mr Stand-Fast-for-Truth. Not rocket science …

Anthology a) A collection, usually of poems by different authors but on a similar theme: for example, *an anthology of war poetry*. Extended to describe other collections, such as an album of songs by various artists. An odd word, in terms of its origins: *antho-* means 'flower', so an *anthology* should be (and occasionally used to be) a collection of flowers. Other words with the same prefix come closer to this root – *anthophilous*, for example, means 'loving flowers' and is used of insects that frequent or feed on flowers. Unless you're among botanists, though, you won't find a lot of use for this arcane piece of knowledge.

Bas-relief b) A form of sculpture in which the subjects – figures, plants or whatever – project slightly from the background, but are attached to it and made of the same material. *Bas* is the French for low; there is also a style called *haut relief* (high relief) in which the subjects stand out much further, not to mention a middle and a shallow version, which for some reason have Italian rather than French names. You can call *bas-relief* low relief if you like; if you want to use the French, remember not to pronounce the *s*.

Bravura a) A brilliant passage or performance, either in music or in theatre. From the Italian, which also gives us *bravado*, it has an implication not just of bravery but of displaying your talents to the utmost.

Chiaroscuro b) An arrangement of light and dark, usually in art but also in photography and cinema, using strong contrast to achieve a striking effect. It's an Italian word meaning 'light dark', pronounced roughly *key-yar-oss-coo-roe*.

Collage b) Miscellaneous bits pasted together on a background to produce an image. The bits can be anything from scraps of cloth and pieces of string to newspaper cuttings and shells – the defining factor is the pasting. From the French *coller*, to stick.

Genre a) A category of literary, musical or artistic work. Religious art, landscape, portraiture and still life could all be described as *genres*, as could country music, reggae and rap, science fiction, crime, horror and romance. A French word meaning kind or sort.

Gouache b) Opaque paint, water-based and mixed with gum or some other sticky substance to make a paste. A French word, pronounced *goo-ash*.

Incunabula a) Early books – a plural, but the singular *incunabulum* is rarely seen. This is a term used by antiquarian booksellers and collectors to denote any printed books produced before 1500. It's from the Latin for *cradle*, because these are books that were produced when printing was in its infancy.

Ingénue c) A young innocent female character, either in a play or in real life. A French word meaning *ingenuous*, naïve and artless.

Juvenilia b) Works belonging to the author's youth, produced before his or her mature style developed. From the Latin for young.

Kabuki b) Japanese theatre – a highly stylized form featuring elaborate costumes, heavy symbolic makeup and exclusively male actors. From Japanese words meaning song, dance and art or skill.

Novella b) A short novel. As simple as that. From Italian.

Palimpsest c) A recycled manuscript, one on which the original writing has been erased and something new written over it. From Ancient Greek words meaning 'rubbed smooth again'.

Pietà a) A depiction of the dead Christ in the arms of his mother, the Virgin Mary, in Christian art. Probably the most famous is by Michelangelo, in St Peter's Basilica in Rome, but it was a popular subject with Renaissance (see page 88) artists. It's the Italian word for pity or compassion, related to the English *piety*.

Art for art's sake

Pseudonym a) A false name, usually one adopted by an author: *Robert Galbraith is a pseudonym of J. K. Rowling*. It's Greek in origin; if you prefer the French equivalent it is *nom de plume* (literally 'pen name').

Repertoire a) All the works a company or performer can perform, whether they are plays, speeches from plays, musical compositions or songs. Two or more plays may also be *in repertoire* or *in repertory*, meaning that they are performed on alternate nights or in short alternating bursts, rather than one running for an extended period before another starts. *Repertoire* is a French word derived from the Latin for a catalogue and *repertory* is from the same root.

Scansion a) The analysis of the metrical structure of verse, working out how it *scans* – that is, what patterns and rules it follows: *the poem echoed the rhythm of galloping horses – scansion of the lines showed a pattern of two short syllables followed by a long one*. From Latin and related to *ultrasound scans* and other modern uses.

Thespian a) An actor. Thespis was an Ancient Greek poet, regarded as the father of tragic drama. Describing an actor as a *thespian* (or *thesp*) is either slightly jokey or slightly disparaging – it suggests they have delusions of grandeur and are perhaps a bit theatrical offstage as well.

Triptych c) A set of three connected paintings, usually forming an altarpiece in Christian art and consisting of three pieces hinged together. From Greek words meaning 'three folds'. You also sometimes see *diptychs*, the same thing but with only two panels.

Words from the Classics

You may know about Jupiter and Juno, Mars and Venus (or their Greek equivalents Zeus and Hera, Ares and Aphrodite), but how well up are you on words that derive from Classical mythology or life in Ancient Greece or Rome?

Bacchanalian a) Drowsy b) Libellous c) Riotous

Basilisk a) A garden plant b) A monster c) A precious stone

Cupidity a) Affection b) Greedy desire c) Sleepiness

Draconian a) Dragon-like b) Excessively strict c) Flowing

Homeric a) Bad-tempered b) Imposing c) Poetic

Junoesque a) Laid back b) Of stately beauty c) Shrew-like, nagging

Laconic a) Lazy b) Mild-mannered c) Using few words

Lucullan a) Gloomy b) Lavish c) Submissive

Mercurial a) Lively b) Miserly c) Productive

Narcissistic a) Permanently sleepy b) Self-obsessed c) Sweet-smelling

Nemesis a) A close friend b) Retribution c) A secretary

Odyssey a) An encyclopedia b) A long journey c) Self-indulgence

Olympian a) Majestic b) Quick-tempered c) Very fast

Peripatetic a) Feeble b) On the outskirts c) Wandering about

Philippic a) A bitter speech b) A love letter c) A time-waster

Sisyphean a) Endless and futile b) Light and airy c) Very loud

Stentorian a) Greedy b) Prone to sneezing c) Very loud

Stygian a) Forgetful b) Gloomy c) Sticky

Titanic a) Doomed b) Huge c) Very strong

Vulcanize a) To explode b) To set fire to c) To treat with sulphur

---

◄ CONFUSABLES ►

aid/aide

Aid is a verb meaning to help or a noun meaning the help that is given: *first aid* and the sort of aid given by a rich country to a poor one are both spelled like this. An *aide* is a person who helps, particularly an unqualified assistant. So *a teaching aide* is someone helping out in the classroom; *a teaching aid* might be a PowerPoint presentation or an abundant supply of crayons.

Answers

~

Bacchanalian c) Riotous, particularly referring to drunken revelry. From Bacchus, the Roman god of wine, fertility and various kinds of excess.

Basilisk b) A monster, specifically a serpent whose look or breath could kill you. It's now the name of a genus of American lizards, but you can also use it in expressions such as *She fixed him with a basilisk eye* – perhaps of a particularly intimidating teacher and a trembling schoolchild.

Cupidity b) Greedy desire. From Cupid, the Roman god of love. *Cupidity* tends to be the desire for money or possessions, though; words to do with sexual desire – *erotic, erotica* and *erogenous zones* – derive from Cupid's Greek equivalent, Eros.

Draconian b) Excessively strict. Draco was an Ancient Athenian law-maker under whose system a staggering number and variety of crimes (from fraud to stealing a cabbage) were punishable by death.

Homeric b) Imposing, on a grand or epic scale, like *The Iliad* and *The Odyssey*, the great works of the poet Homer. The word doesn't have to refer to poetry: you can have *a Homeric struggle* or, if you are feeling *bacchanalian* (see above), *a Homeric drinking session*.

Junoesque b) Of stately beauty. Juno was the queen of the Roman gods and women likened to her are likely to be on the large side, but elegant and regal in their bearing.

Laconic c) Using few words. Laconia was a province of Ancient Greece; its capital was Sparta. The Spartans had more time for military discipline than for the arts – hence the word *spartan*, meaning disciplined and austere. They also had no time for wasting words. There is a famous story that Philip of Macedon, father of Alexander the Great, was planning to invade. 'If I enter Laconia,' he wrote to their leaders, 'I shall raze Sparta to the ground.' Back came the one-word, *laconic* reply: 'If.'

Lucullan b) Lavish, after a wealthy Roman called Lucullus, famous for the extravagant banquets he gave.

Mercurial a) Lively, volatile, subject to quick changes of mood. Mercury was the messenger of the Roman gods, prone to flitting about all over the place. He was also the god of merchants, travellers, thieves and rogues – so someone with *a mercurial temperament* is likely to be fun but not entirely reliable.

Narcissistic b) Self-obsessed. Narcissus was a beautiful but vain youth in Greek mythology. Catching sight of his own reflection in a pool, he fell instantly in love and, receiving no encouragement from the object of his affections, pined away, turning into the flower that now bears his name.

Nemesis b) Retribution, from the Greek goddess of vengeance. *A nemesis* can also be the person or thing that brings about another's downfall – as Sherlock Holmes was to Moriarty, for example.

Odyssey b) A long journey, from the travels of Odysseus or Ulysses, in Homer's poem *The Odyssey*. It took the Greek hero ten years to get home from the Trojan War and he had many adventures (and mistresses) on the way. A modern odyssey needn't have mistresses, but it should be long, adventurous and more complicated than just going from A to B.

Olympian a) Majestic, godlike in attitude. Mount Olympus was the home of the Greek gods, so anyone who behaves in an *Olympian manner* is far removed from day-to-day concerns. You might also *descend from Olympian heights* if, at the end of a formal speech, you blurted out, 'Will you lot just shut up and listen!' Mount Olympus was nowhere near Olympia, where the first Olympic Games were held, though, confusingly, someone who competes in the games today is known as an *Olympian*.

Peripatetic c) Wandering about, itinerant, often in the sense of having more than one job or post, or of needing to seek work in more than one place: *a peripatetic violin teacher* might visit several schools, because teaching the violin isn't a full-time job in any of them. From the school of philosophy founded in Ancient Athens by Aristotle, who used to teach while wandering about (as opposed to the Stoics, who sat under a *stoa* or porch – see page 26).

Philippic a) A bitter speech of denunciation or accusation. From the town of Philippi in Macedonia, named after the Philip mentioned under *laconic*, above, against whom the Greek orator Demosthenes directed some vitriolic speeches in the fourth century BC. Three hundred years later, the Roman orator Cicero directed similar speeches against Mark Antony, who conveniently had recently fought two battles at Philippi.

Sisyphean a) Endless and futile. Sisyphus, punished by the gods for arrogance, was condemned throughout eternity to push a boulder up a hill; the moment it neared the top it would roll back down and he would have to start again. A modern *Sisyphean task* may involve dealing with mountains of paperwork rather than boulders, but the feeling that you will achieve nothing, however hard you try, is the same as it was in ancient times.

Stentorian c) Very loud; from Stentor, the Greek herald with a powerful voice.

Stygian b) Gloomy. In Greek mythology, the dead crossed the River Styx in order to enter the Underworld. A *Stygian oath* – one sworn in the name of the river and the goddess in charge of it – was inviolable, even for the gods, but today the word normally conjures up the darkness of the waters and the general hellishness of the place through which they flowed. In this looser sense purists would still insist on the initial capital, but (as with most of the words in this section) you can get away without it.

Titanic c) Very strong, as in *a titanic struggle*. Named after the Titans, a race of gods in early Greek mythology.

Vulcanize c) To treat with sulphur or sulphur compounds under heat and pressure – something you do to rubber to make it stronger and more flexible. From *Vulcan*, the Roman god of fire, after whom *volcanoes* are named. He was also the god of blacksmiths and metalworkers, said to have his forge underneath Mount Etna in Sicily and to be responsible for its rumblings.

B is for ...

There's no reason why words beginning with B should be more interesting than any others (and the next section, on words beginning with F, should bear this out), but here are a few that are quite fun.

Badinage a) Light-hearted chatter b) Promiscuous behaviour c) A quick, thoughtless decision

Baize a) A cooking sauce b) A sea mist c) A woollen fabric

Ballistic To do with ... a) lending money b) the path of a missile c) seamanship

Balsam a) A fragrant ointment b) Nonsense c) A slow, stately dance

Bandana a) An Australian tree b) A head or neck scarf c) A Spanish dance

Bandicoot a) A marsupial b) A skirt c) A water bird

Banshee a) Money given to a beggar b) An ominous spirit c) A slick sales pitch

Banyan a) A fruit b) A mushroom c) A tree

Bargee a) A barrier b) An obsolete coin c) Someone who works on a barge

Bastion a) A chore b) A fortification c) A killjoy

Bellwether a) A headscarf b) A leader c) A storm at sea

Beriberi a) A disease b) A poisonous fruit c) A tropical bird

Bevel a) To cut at an angle b) To dance c) To rejoice

Bigotry a) Extravagance b) Intolerance c) Swearing

Blewits a) A culinary herb b) A disease of cattle c) A mushroom

Bludgeon a) To blur, smudge b) To caution c) To strike heavily

Brusque a) Abrupt b) Orderly, disciplined c) Run-down, shabby

Bucolic a) Drunken b) Elegant c) Rustic

Burlesque a) A dance move b) An imitation or send-up
c) A sturdy build

Byzantine a) Captivating, delightful b) Immensely complicated
c) Out of date

Answers

Badinage a) Light-hearted chatter, a combination of the witty and the frivolous: *the office badinage could be irritating, but it was better than discussing politics or sport.*

Baize c) A woollen fabric, usually green and seen on the top of billiard/snooker/pool tables.

Ballistic b) To do with the path of a missile. The science of *ballistics* studies the forces of propulsion, aerodynamics, gravity and other factors to work out where a bullet or a missile is going to land. A *ballistic missile* is, to quote the *OED*, 'powered (as a rocket) and guided only in the initial phase of its flight, thereafter falling freely towards its target, typically following a high, arching trajectory'. So in the latter part of its flight it is not under control and may go – well, anywhere. Hence the figurative use, *to go ballistic*, which initially meant to go haywire but soon developed into losing one's temper and/or becoming uncontrollably enthusiastic about something. Loss of control is the defining factor.

Balsam a) A fragrant ointment or medicine, obtained from various shrubs and trees. The name of that fashionable condiment *balsamic vinegar* is a translation from the Italian and meant originally that it was restorative or curative. *Balsam* itself can be traced back to a Hebrew word for spice, so fragrance is the key feature here.

Bandana b) A head or neck scarf, sometimes spelled *bandanna*. An Indian invention and a Hindi word, it was traditionally made of silk, brightly coloured and tie-dyed to leave some patches white or pale. Nowadays, you can find bandanas in cotton, in black and white, and often in Paisley patterns – a design that originated in Persia and was first mass-produced in Scotland. Plenty to upset the purists there.

Bandicoot a) A marsupial, native to Australia and New Guinea, rather rat-like but with a long pointed nose, upright ears and powerful hind legs like a rabbit's. The name comes from Telugu, a language of India in which *pandi* means 'pig'; it has nothing to do with *bandy* in the sense of either striped or bow-legged. A *coot* is a water bird, but doesn't come in a *bandy* or *bandi-* variety.

Banshee b) An ominous female spirit in Irish folklore who wails to announce an impending death. In casual use, *howling like a banshee* could describe anyone making a lot of unpleasant noise. Money given to a beggar in Persian-speaking circles is *baksheesh* (see page 143).

Banyan c) A tree of the fig family, common in India and intriguing because its branches drop shoots to the ground, where they take root and support the original growth. Older specimens therefore cover an impressively large area.

Bargee c) Someone who works on a barge. The *OED* tells us austerely that 'the suffix is employed apparently arbitrarily': words ending in *-ee* are usually formed from a verb rather than a noun (*employee*, someone who is employed; *standee*, someone who is obliged to stand). Nevertheless, *bargee* is found in Samuel Pepys' diaries of the 1660s and seems to be hanging on wherever there are barges to be worked on. *Bargeman* is even older, but *bargee* has the advantage of being unisex.

Bastion b) A fortification, specifically one that projects from the wall of a castle enabling anyone in it to fire to the sides as well as to the front. In figurative use, a *bastion* is someone or something that upholds a principle, particularly one that is in danger of ceasing to exist – *the last bastion of liberal democracy*, to pick an example at random.

Bellwether b) A leader, particularly one that is followed mindlessly. *Wether* is an old word for a castrated ram, so the *bellwether* – a wether wearing a bell – encourages the other members of the flock to follow in his tinkling footsteps and helps the shepherd to keep track of them. In non-sheep-related use, a *bellwether* is often a political trend: *the results in Ohio were a bellwether of what was to happen nationwide*.

Beriberi a) A disease, caused by a deficiency of vitamin B1 and characterized by pain, paralysis and swelling of the limbs. Not nice. Eat your beans.

Bevel a) To cut at an angle, so that two *bevelled* pieces come together on a diagonal rather than at a right angle. Windows and mirrors often feature bevelled frames.

Bigotry b) Intolerance of ideas other than your own, particularly when it comes to race, colour and/or creed. Those who indulge in *bigotry* are *bigots* – narrow-minded, unreasonable and generally unpleasant people. The word seems to have been an insult applied to the Normans by the French nearly a thousand years ago; it may be a French mispronunciation of *by God*, but no one is entirely sure.

Blewits c) A mushroom of the genus *Lepista*, with a brown cap and blue stalk. The name probably comes from the colour, and although the singular is strictly speaking *blewits*, the more obvious *blewit* is widely used.

Bludgeon c) To strike heavily – originally with a *bludgeon*, a solid, blunt club. In less violent circles, *to bludgeon* is to bully someone into doing something against their will: *I didn't want to volunteer, but I was bludgeoned into it.*

Brusque a) Abrupt, short and curt in speech and manner: *I thought it was a reasonable request, but a brusque 'No' was all the reply I got.*

Bucolic c) Rustic: referring to a landscape or a way of life that is perceived as being slower and less sophisticated than an urban one. From the Greek for a herdsman, though nowadays *a bucolic pastime* is just as likely to be watching cricket on a village green as it is to be keeping an eye on sheep or goats.

Burlesque b) An imitation, a send-up or satire of a work in a more serious literary or dramatic style. The great Spanish novel *Don Quixote* is a *burlesque* of novels of chivalry; the Austin Powers movies are *burlesques* of the spy genre. What is sometimes called *American burlesque* began as a form of variety show that included satirical comedy but became better known for its striptease acts. The word comes via French from Italian, where *burla* means a jest or a piece of nonsense.

Byzantine b) Immensely complicated, from a highly decorated and stylized form of religious art and architecture that developed in Byzantium (now Istanbul) from about the fourth century AD: think mosaics, minarets, fancy brickwork and lots of bright colours. In that context it is usually spelled with a capital; go into lower case and *byzantine* can be applied to rules and regulations, arguments, office hierarchies – anything unnecessarily intricate but strictly enforced.

Three of a kind

It's a common complaint that English is difficult to learn, mostly because of the oddities of our spelling (why don't *bough*, *cough*, *rough* and *through* rhyme?) and the number of lookalikes and sound-alikes we have (see the various examples scattered through this book). It doesn't help that we have a number of words that have not just two but three or more meanings.

Draw can be the way you create a picture, it can be the end of a sporting match when the scores are equal or it can be what you do when you pull curtains closed. From that last sense of pulling gently, we have the figurative uses of *drawing your own conclusions* or *drawing someone out* by encouraging them to talk about themselves. They all come ultimately from the same source – an Old English word that also gave us *drag*.

Hock is a white wine, named after Hochheim in Germany. It's part of an animal's leg, equivalent to the human ankle, from an Old English word. And it means to pawn – to give something, usually to a pawnbroker, as security when they lend you money – derived from a Dutch word for prison.

Lay is what hens do to eggs and what you do to the table before a meal (Old English); it's an old word for a song or narrative poem, as in Walter Scott's *Lay of the Last Minstrel* (Old French); and, as we saw on page 61, it means 'not clerical, not connected with the Church' (also Old French, but not the same word).

Moor is a heath, an expanse of open ground (Old English); it's a way of tying up a boat (a different Old English source); and it's a member of a North African race whose name derives from Latin via French.

Pink is a colour and a flower related to the carnation; it means to trim a fabric (with *pinking shears*) so as to produce a wavy edge that won't fray; and it is also to stab someone lightly with a sword. All of uncertain origin.

Snipe is a marsh bird with a long straight bill – another name of uncertain origin, but it gave rise to the idea of a *sniper*, someone who shoots a gun from a hidden position, which in turn gave us *to snipe* at someone, to rebuke them unkindly.

F is for ...

... nothing remotely improper. Just twenty interesting words that happen to share an initial letter. Musical instruments or types of wheat? Giving generously or teetering unsteadily? You decide.

Fallible a) Capable of making a mistake b) Dishonest c) Dizzy

Farrago a) A dance b) A mixture, a muddle c) A type of wheat

Fascia a) A bundle b) The flat surface above a shop window c) A purse or handbag

Fastidious a) Hard to please b) Quick-tempered c) Sober

Filigree a) Delicate ornamentation b) A flight of steps c) A shrub

Fillip a) A breed of horse b) A pane of glass c) A stimulant

Flaunt a) To flatter b) To move impatiently c) To show off

Fluctuate a) To hiccup b) To leak c) To vary

Flugelhorn a) A breed of sheep b) A head-dress c) A musical instrument

Fluorescent a) Emitting heat b) Emitting light c) Emitting liquid

Foible a) A lie b) A stupid action c) A weakness

Fractious a) Easily broken b) Generous c) Irritable

Freeload a) To donate to charity b) To rely on someone's generosity c) To smuggle

Friable a) Crumbly b) Redeemable, able to be saved c) Resistant to high heat

Frieze a) A cargo b) A decorative band c) A tablecloth

Fugue a) A cavern b) A fleeting moment c) A piece of music

Fulminate a) To balance b) To criticize angrily c) To explain, throw light on

Funicular a) A fairground attraction b) A hillside railway c) A type of mushroom

Fuselage a) The body of an aircraft b) A firework c) A joint in woodwork

Futon a) A Chinese jacket b) A Japanese bed c) A Spanish sword

Answers

Fallible a) Capable of making a mistake. The *infallibility* of the Pope is a dogma of the Catholic Church, and oddly enough *infallible* is more commonly used than its opposite. *I don't claim to be infallible, but ...* is something you might say when you were claiming to be right this time.

Farrago b) A mixture, a muddle. From an old word meaning the mash that is fed to cattle, but now more often used metaphorically: *a farrago of nonsense* or *a farrago of lies*.

Fascia b) The flat surface above a shop window on which its name, phone number and/or promotional slogans are displayed. The first syllable is pronounced *face* and the word is loosely related to the Latin for a bundle of rods from which we also get *Fascism*.

Fastidious a) Hard to please, eager to find fault or to complain about details. It isn't necessarily an insult, but it's borderline. *A fastidious dresser* could simply be smart and well-groomed; *a fastidious eater* is likely to be the annoying person who leaves potato skins on the side of the plate.

Filigree a) Delicate ornamentation, usually of metalwork or lace: *a filigree brooch* might be made from thin wires of gold or silver twisted together. From the Latin for thread, which also appears in *file* (because in early filing systems documents were hung from threads) and *filament*.

Fillip c) A stimulant, something bracing or cheering that gives you a new burst of energy: *I was struggling with my thesis, but her praise gave me a real fillip*. Bizarrely, *fillip* originally meant the gesture of snapping the fingers and the word is said to imitate that sound. I say bizarrely because when I snap my fingers the sound it makes is definitely one syllable and sounds more like – well, *snap*.

Flaunt c) To show off, to display ostentatiously. A disapproving word: *she's really flaunting her figure in that tight dress* or *he didn't have to flaunt* *his exam results in front of me when he knew I'd done badly.* To move impatiently, particularly when leaving the room in a huff, is to *flounce.*

Fluctuate c) To vary, to move in an unstable way: *the doctor was worried by the way her heartbeat was fluctuating* or *public opinion seems to fluctuate depending on what day of the week the poll is taken.* From the Latin for a wave.

Flugelhorn c) A musical instrument, a bit like a trumpet but generally warmer in tone, popular in brass bands. *Flügel* is the German for 'wing' or 'flank' and the name apparently comes from the fact that a forerunner of this instrument was used in hunting in eighteenth-century Germany to direct the flanks of the hunt.

Fluorescent b) Emitting light, as from a *fluorescent tube*, one of those long tubes used to provide bright light in work areas. The scientific explanation is a complicated one involving mercury, phosphor and ultraviolet, but the derivation of the word is the Latin for flow or flux.

Foible c) A weakness in character or habits, related to *feeble.* Slightly worse than a *quirk* (see page 62), which is merely a peculiarity; *foible* contains a gentle criticism: *she had a foible of talking loudly to herself and being rude about everyone in the room.*

Fractious c) Irritable, easily annoyed. This could describe a person, particularly a small child: *she's a bit fractious tonight; she has another tooth coming through.* Or it could be applied to a situation: *we had a fractious weekend – it was too wet to go out and we all got on each other's nerves.* Ultimately from the Latin for break, related to *fraction* and *fracture.*

Freeload b) To rely on someone's generosity, but in a bad way: to sponge off them and expect them to pay for everything: *if I hadn't insisted that I needed the spare room as an office, he would have freeloaded off me all summer.*

Friable a) Crumbly. A word used enthusiastically by gardeners to describe just the right sort of soil, neither too wet nor too dry, too rich nor too barren.

Frieze b) A decorative band, such as the carvings above the columns in a Classical temple or the patterned strip around the walls of a room that is otherwise plainly painted. From *Phrygia*, an ancient region in what is now Turkey, famous for its decorative gold embroidery.

Fugue c) A piece of music, defined by experts as 'a polyphonic composition constructed on one or more short subjects or themes, which are harmonized according to the laws of counterpoint, and introduced from time to time with various contrapuntal devices'. Clear? Good. The word has also been adopted by psychiatry to describe a state of mind (a *fugue state*) in which the sufferer loses their memory temporarily and flees from their own identity. From the Latin for to flee, related to *fugitive*.

Fulminate b) To criticize angrily, to thunder against: *my grandfather was always fulminating against the morals of the younger generation*. Funny, really, because it comes from the Latin for lightning.

Funicular b) A hillside railway, operated by cables passing round a driving wheel at the summit. From the Latin for a thin cord, though in modern usage you don't want it to be *too* thin.

Fuselage a) The body of an aircraft – the torso, as it were, as opposed to the wings and tail. From a French word for spindle, because of its shape.

Futon b) A Japanese bed, or strictly speaking the quilt that is laid on the floor to serve as a bed. From the Japanese, but you probably realized that.

Words with contradictory meanings

As if having words with more than two meanings wasn't bad enough (see page 134), here we have a handful whose meanings actually contradict each other: they're known as *contronyms*.

To cleave to something is to cling to it tightly, but *to cleave* can also mean to split something in two.

To clip is to fasten together (as with a paper clip) or to cut a bit off (as with a haircut).

Fast means moving quickly, but it also means tied tightly so that you can't move at all (and, in similar vein, *to bound* is to leap like an antelope, while *to be bound* or *bound up* is to be tied so that you can't possibly bound).

Finished means completed and ready to be used, as in *a finished product*; it also means past it, done for and no longer able to be used: *his prospects of becoming a doctor are finished now that he has failed his exams*.

Left means departed – *he left in a hurry* – or remaining behind – *I was left staring after him*.

To sanction something is to permit it, to give it your blessing: *I couldn't possibly sanction your staying out so late*. In a political sense, though, *sanctions* are more likely to be prohibitions: *for many years, the United States imposed sanctions on trade with Cuba*.

Go figure.

Words from Asian languages

Ever since Europeans started to trade with countries to the east – from the Arabic-speaking lands through India to Malaya (as it once was), China and Japan – English has picked up words from the local languages. How many of these do you know?

Algorithm a) A drumbeat b) A measure of pain c) A procedure

Asana a) Chinese calligraphy b) The Japanese art of flower arranging c) A yoga posture

Baksheesh a) An Asian donkey b) A command to an animal c) Money given as a tip

Bonsai The Japanese art of … a) flower arranging b) miniature gardening c) paper folding

Cushy a) Comfortable b) Juicy c) Soft and squashy, like a cushion

Doolally a) Crazy b) Excessively cheerful c) Unwashed

Gung-ho a) Keen to be involved b) Loud c) Pretentious

Haiku a) A ceremonial tea party b) Poetry c) Ritual cleansing

Honcho a) The boss b) A canteen worker c) A secretary or aide

Juggernaut a) A large vehicle b) A martial art c) A musical instrument

Kamikaze a) Comfortable b) Eaten raw c) Suicidal

Karma a) Fate b) Meditation c) Sorrow

Kowtow a) To bow b) To gossip c) To practise a martial art

Manga a) A comic b) A long sleeve c) A sash

Nabob a) A chutney b) A hut c) A wealthy man

Pariah a) A crocodile b) An outcast c) A small tiger

Pundit a) An expert b) A hut c) A sacred text

Purdah a) Meditation b) Petty theft c) Seclusion

Samurai a) A form of poetry b) A style of theatre c) A warrior

Sashimi a) Raw fish b) A room with paper walls c) A tea ceremony

Answers

Algorithm c) A procedure or set of rules in maths or computing. You (or more probably your machine) follow the various steps of an algorithm in order to solve a problem or perform a task. The word's origins can be traced back to the name of an early Arabian mathematician with a little bit of the Greek-derived *arithmetic* thrown in.

Asana c) A yoga posture, traditionally the sitting posture used in meditation. Like many terms in yoga, this comes from the ancient Indian language Sanskrit.

Baksheesh c) Money given as a tip or as a present to a beggar. From the Persian.

Bonsai b) The Japanese art of miniature gardening, producing tiny trees and shrubs in pots or trays. Flower arranging is *ikebana* and paper folding *origami*.

Cushy a) Comfortable, easy, particularly with reference to an undemanding job (*a cushy number*, in old-fashioned slang). From a Hindi word that is nothing to do with cushions.

Doolally a) Crazy. Deolali, a town near Mumbai, was, in the nineteenth century, a transit camp for British soldiers. Time spent there was so unpleasant and boring that many occupants 'went Deolali', meaning they lost their mind.

Gung-ho a) Keen to be involved, originally in a military operation, and often dashing in with more enthusiasm than preparation. From the Mandarin Chinese for 'to work together', but with less common sense than that expression implies.

Haiku b) A form of Japanese poetry consisting of three lines and a total of seventeen syllables. (If you aren't familiar with it, Google it: it's surprising what you can say, and how beautifully, in so few words.)

Honcho a) The boss, literally Japanese for 'squad chief'. In English, people often say *head honcho* – unnecessary and annoying, but probably too thoroughly entrenched to go away.

Juggernaut a) A large vehicle, originally one involved in a Hindu ceremony in which pilgrims threw themselves under its wheels. Hence a huge lorry and also, say, a vast government department that moves relentlessly along its own path, brushing aside or crushing anything that attempts to stop it.

Kamikaze c) Suicidal, from the Second World War Japanese planes that crashed, loaded with explosives, into enemy targets. The sense quickly extended to include the pilots of such planes and the word is now more generally used for anyone or anything particularly reckless: *the kamikaze motorcycle messengers dealing with the rush-hour traffic*. Literally 'wind of the spirits', with reference to the powerful winds (believed to have been sent by benevolent spirits) that in the thirteenth century destroyed a Mongol fleet that was attempting to invade Japan. The Second World War use was a piece of propaganda, suggesting that the planes were like divine winds, once more beating back an enemy.

Karma a) Fate. Another Sanskrit word, conveying the Hindu and Buddhist concept of retribution, of both good and bad deeds coming back to reward or haunt us.

Kowtow a) To bow or defer to someone, particularly in a cringing, abject sort of way. From the Japanese for bowing until your forehead touched the floor.

Manga a) A comic or graphic novel, originally Japanese, designed to appeal to adults as well as teenagers.

Nabob c) A wealthy man, originally a European who went to India and made his fortune. From the Hindi and related to *nawab*, a local ruler.

Pariah b) An outcast, originally a member of a lowly caste in India. The Indian crocodile is a *gharial* or *gavial*.

Pundit a) An expert – often, now, one who appears on television expressing views on the political or economic situation or on a sporting event. From a Hindi word meaning learned or skilled.

Purdah c) Seclusion, specifically the sort of seclusion that keeps women hidden away from the world's prying eyes, but now also used in a less formal sense: *he went into purdah for a while until the scandal died down.* From a Hindu word for a veil.

Samurai c) A warrior, a member of an aristocratic Japanese class until the nineteenth century.

Sashimi a) Raw fish (or sometimes meat), thinly sliced and served with soy sauce. Japanese.

CONFUSABLES

eminent/imminent

An *eminent* academic (or lawyer or politician or whatever) is distinguished and stands out from his or her colleagues. Such a person may also show *eminent good sense* or *eminent ability* – their good sense or their ability is outstanding and obvious. *Imminent* means likely to happen soon: if *their departure is imminent,* they are putting their coats on and thanking you for your hospitality.

Words from African languages

―――――〜―――――

This is a bit of a catch-all section: some of the words are Arabic, but with connections to Egypt; some come from Afrikaans, the Dutch-based language of early South African colonists. Others are Swahili or various other languages of the African continent; still others originated in Africa but came into English via the slave population of the Caribbean and the Southern United States. So, African in the broadest sense…

Adobe a) A brick b) A herb c) A stew

Ankh a) A cross b) A headscarf c) A small pyramid

Basenji a) A Central African dog b) A South African tree c) A West African dance

Biltong a) Dried meat b) A hut c) A song

Boomslang a) A snake b) A sudden noise c) A weapon

Bwana a) An antelope b) A lizard c) A term of respect

Dengue a) A dwelling b) A fever c) A musical instrument

Gumbo a) A musical instrument b) A stew c) A wild dog

Kraal a) A battle b) A cereal crop c) An enclosure

Loofah a) A small primate b) A sponge c) A sweet

Macaque a) A cloth b) A monkey c) A musical instrument

Safari a) Carelessness, lack of anxiety b) Goodwill c) A hunting expedition

Sjambok a) An antelope b) A meeting c) A whip

Spoor a) A raid b) A trail c) A village

Trek a) A biscuit b) A journey c) A parcel of land

Tsetse a) A fly b) A tree c) A wild horse

Veld a) An animal skin b) A fruit pudding c) Open grassland

Voodoo a) A bird b) A religious cult c) A small mammal

Vuvuzela a) An antelope b) A cloak c) A horn

Zombie a) A corpse brought back to life b) A spicy dish c) A tablecloth

Answers

Adobe a) A brick made from mud dried in the sun, widely used for building in Africa, the Middle East and Central America. The finest examples of adobe architecture are found among the Dogon people of Mali in West Africa, though there is no shortage in Santa Fe, New Mexico. Originally from Arabic and pronounced as three syllables: *a-doh-bee* or *a-doo-bee*.

Ankh a) A cross, used in Egyptian hieroglyphics as a symbol of life and also in the Coptic Christian art of north-eastern Africa. From an Egyptian word meaning life or soul.

Basenji a) A Central African dog, best known for its inability to bark. (It isn't silent, though – it can yodel with the best of them.) The name was also applied to an African who refused, in colonial times, to convert to Christianity or to adopt other European customs; it comes from a local word meaning indigenous or wild.

Biltong a) Dried meat, cured, spiced and cut into strips; eaten as a snack in southern Africa. From Dutch words meaning 'strip of rump'.

Boomslang a) A snake, tree-dwelling and poisonous. An Afrikaans name meaning 'tree snake'.

Bwana c) A term of respect, the Swahili for *mister* or *sir*.

Dengue b) A fever transmitted by mosquitoes, with symptoms including headaches, joint pain and skin rash. Pronounced as two syllables – *deng-ee*; brought into English via Cuban Spanish, but probably originally from Swahili.

Gumbo b) A stew or soup made from okra (often known as ladies' fingers); also a colloquial name for the vegetable itself. Originally from a Bantu word, it came into English via the French of Louisiana.

Words from African languages

Kraal c) An enclosure for livestock in South Africa; also, a village surrounded by a fence. An Afrikaans word related to *corral*.

Loofah b) A sponge, in the sense of something you wash with. Biologically it's a vine, belonging to the genus *Luffa*. The gourd-like fruit has fibrous insides which, when dried, are used for bathing or scrubbing. Originally an Egyptian Arabic word.

Macaque b) A monkey, various species of which are found across Asia, Africa and Gibraltar, but whose name comes from a West African word meaning (unsurprisingly) monkey.

Safari c) A hunting expedition or one undertaken for the purposes of scientific research, usually covering a long distance. More recently, it's come to be used of a type of holiday in which tourists see and photograph wildlife without feeling the need to shoot it. A Swahili word.

Sjambok c) A whip made from rhinoceros or hippopotamus hide. As the *OED* delicately puts it, it is *used in South Africa for driving cattle and sometimes for administering chastisement.* From Afrikaans, but oddly it traces its origins back to Persian and Urdu; it therefore isn't from the same root as *springbok*, *gemsbok* and other African antelopes, the end of whose names is related to the English *buck*.

Spoor b) A trail, particularly signs such as footprints or dung that enable trackers to follow wild animals. Afrikaans again.

Trek b) A journey, usually a long and difficult one. Also from Afrikaans.

Tsetse a) A fly, notorious for spreading the disease known as sleeping sickness. From Tswana (the language of Botswana) and pronounced *tset-see* or *tseet-see*.

Veld c) Open grassland in southern Africa, sometimes spelled *veldt*. Originally from a Dutch word for field and comparable to *pampas*, *prairie*, *steppe* or *savanna(h)* in other parts of the world.

Voodoo b) A religious cult involving witchcraft and going into a trance in order to communicate with spirits; it developed in West Africa and spread to Haiti and other parts of the Caribbean, and to the southern United States. *Voodoo* is also used loosely as a verb meaning 'to put a curse on someone' or 'to bring bad luck'. From a West African language.

Vuvuzela c) A horn that produces a loud monotone sound, much used by enthusiastic members of the crowd at South African sporting events. Possibly from a Zulu word.

Zombie a) A corpse brought back to life, originally as a result of West African witchcraft, latterly as a feature of many a scary movie. From a West African word for a magical object.

Words that express disapproval

Want to be unpleasant? Tell someone off in style? Then there's nothing that will make you feel better than getting your words right. Here are a few to choose from.

Asperity a) Miserliness b) Shamelessness c) Sharpness

Bombastic a) Excessively loud b) Extravagant c) Unfriendly

Churlish a) Distasteful b) Greedy c) Ungracious

Contentious a) Controversial b) Ungracious c) Unnecessary

Derisory a) Mocking b) Ridiculously small c) Tastelessly showy

Effrontery a) Carelessness b) Cheek c) Pretentiousness

Feckless a) Disgraceful b) Irresponsible c) Promiscuous

Iniquitous a) Extravagant b) Overly curious c) Wicked

Lascivious a) Greedy b) Lazy c) Lustful

Mercenary a) Lustful b) Obsessed with money c) Short-tempered

Meretricious a) Promiscuous b) Superficially attractive c) Unreliable

Noisome a) Offensively loud b) Unpleasant smelling c) Valueless

Obstreperous a) Promiscuous b) Unpleasant smelling c) Unruly

Parsimonious a) Hypocritically religious b) Mean c) Sulky

Peevish a) Disloyal b) Mean c) Pettily irritable

Perfidious a) Lazy b) Mean c) Treacherous

Pusillanimous a) Cowardly b) Insincere c) Unhygienic

Rapacious a) Grasping b) Hypocritical c) Unfriendly

Scurrilous a) Abusive b) Dirty c) Grovelling

Truculent a) Disagreeable b) Pompous c) Shameless

Answers

Asperity c) Sharpness, especially in speech: *He spoke with some asperity – he was annoyed and he wanted everyone to know it.*

Bombastic b) Extravagant in speech or language. Nothing to do with bombs, *bombast* was once a material used for stuffing or padding, so *bombastic* meant literally stuffed or figuratively inflated, using fancier words (and more of them, possibly using them more loudly) than necessary.

Churlish c) Ungracious, like a *churl*, an uneducated country person. This dates back to the time when it was assumed that country folk *were* generally uneducated and that city people had better manners (hence *urbane*, related to *urban*).

Contentious a) Controversial, like a *bone of contention*, something to be argued over.

Derisory b) Ridiculously small, particularly a sum of money: *I was offered a derisory pay rise. Derisive* means mocking.

Effrontery b) Cheek, insolence: *he had the effrontery to cry off at the last minute, when he must have known for weeks he wasn't going to come.*

Feckless b) Irresponsible, lacking in *feck*, an old word meaning substance: *he was charming but feckless, unable to hold down a job and hopeless at providing for his family.*

Iniquitous c) Wicked and unjust – *an iniquitous decision* is intolerable, unfair and probably the result of a cover-up. Overly curious is *inquisitive*.

Lascivious c) Lustful. For some reason, we have a number of words beginning with *l* that all mean much the same thing – *lewd, lubricious* and *libidinous* are three more. This one is from a Latin word that originally meant playful, but came to mean playful in a very particular – and not very pleasant – sense. The *c* isn't pronounced, so the word is *lassivious* rather than *laskivious*.

Mercenary b) Obsessed with money. A *mercenary person* will count every penny he or she has to spend, while a *mercenary soldier* (or just a *mercenary*) will fight for anyone who pays enough, regardless of the rights and wrongs of the cause.

Meretricious b) Superficially attractive, from the Latin for a prostitute, but now usually meaning plausible but false (*a meretricious argument*) or alluring but lacking in substance (*the meretricious charms of the latest nightclub*).

Noisome b) Unpleasant smelling or offensive in a more general way: *the alley was particularly noisome on a Sunday, as the bins weren't emptied until Monday morning*. Related not to *noise* but to *annoyance*.

Obstreperous c) Unruly, unwilling to submit to discipline – the word from which we developed *stroppy*.

Parsimonious b) Mean, stingy, grasping, Scrooge-like. If you thought *mercenary* was bad (see above), think again. From a Latin word meaning to save or be sparing.

Peevish c) Pettily irritable, complaining in a childish way: *she's always peevish in the car; today she started whining before we'd reached the end of the road*. Of unknown origin, or perhaps no one wants to own up to it.

Perfidious c) Treacherous, likely to break a promise. The central part of the word comes from the Latin for faith, which also gives us *fidelity* – a quality in which a perfidious person is utterly lacking.

Pusillanimous a) Cowardly, from the Latin for weak-spirited. Despite its derivation, this is a strong word: *pusillanimity* is real shaking-in-your-shoes patheticness, not just being a bit hesitant.

Rapacious a) Grasping, like a *raptor* or bird of prey, though a rapacious person is usually more interested in money than in small rodents.

Scurrilous a) Abusive, defamatory, particularly in a coarsely joking way: *the papers are printing scurrilous rumours about his private life*. From the Latin for a buffoon; nothing to do with *scurrying*.

Truculent a) Disagreeable. Possibly a bit *churlish*, but also inclined to be *obstreperous* (see above).

Emerging scathed ...

Feckless and *hapless* (see pages 153 and 181) aren't the only words not to have opposites in daily use. P. G. Wodehouse's much-quoted *if not actually disgruntled, he was far from being gruntled* is funny because we know (and we know that Wodehouse knows) that although *disgruntled* is a perfectly normal, everyday word for *discontented*, its opposite isn't a 'real word' – Wodehouse's is the first citation in the *OED* and later uses are obviously humorous and inspired by him.

Another word that doesn't exist is *combobulated*. *Discombobulated* is a comical word for upset or perturbed and, as with *disgruntled*, we recognize the prefix *dis-* as creating an opposite: it crops up in *disown*, to deny owning, *displace*, to move out of place, and so on. But various nineteenth-century American journalists apparently came up with *discombobulated* as an alternative to *discomposed* or *discomfited*, because it sounded both funny and suitably confused. In the early days, *discomboberated* and *discombobracated* are also found, suggesting that their creators were just messing about and waiting for one version or another to take hold.

There are many more. *Dishevelled* comes from the French meaning stripped of hair; now it normally means that your hair, and probably your clothes too, are untidy and all over the place. But when did you last hear of someone well-groomed being described as *shevelled*? Or indeed *kempt* as opposed to *unkempt*? Or *couth*, rather than *uncouth*, if they have civilized manners? It can work the other way, too: someone whose appearance is *impeccable* is impossible to fault; but if they look dishevelled you don't normally describe them as *peccable*.

We have *inchoate* (see page 181) but not *choate*; *disconsolate* but not *consolate*; *nondescript* but not *descript*; *unscathed* but not *scathed*; *nonsensical* but not *sensical*. There's no linguistic reason for any of this – these non-words or rarely used words could easily become ... well, just *words* if enough people used them. Have a go. You could start a new trend, as long as you aren't too *bashful* about it. Perhaps you should be *bashless* instead.

Good, bad or indifferent

Good-tempered or bad? Or just not bothered? Pleasant, unpleasant or something in between?

Acrimonious a) Bitter b) Complaining c) Delaying

Anathema a) Judgement b) A long, tedious journey c) Something hateful

Anodyne a) Dull b) Horrible c) Unhygienic

Antipathy a) Dislike b) Indifference c) Tactlessness

Apathetic a) Boring b) Not bothered c) Suffering

Cacophony a) Absurdity b) Conceitedness c) An unpleasant noise

Curmudgeon a) A grumpy person b) A slave c) A tyrant

Dysfunctional a) Abnormal b) Antisocial c) Noisy

Eugenics The study of … a) good pronunciation b) methods of 'improving' the human race c) intelligence

Hidebound a) Enthusiastic b) Restricted by petty rules c) Secretive

Impunity a) Cruelty b) A lack of unpleasant consequences c) Neutrality

Insouciant a) Carefree b) Ill-mannered c) Suspicious

Intransigent a) Agitated b) Fierce c) Unbending

Magnanimous a) Boastful b) Generous c) Splendid, lavish

Nefarious a) Mumbling b) Unnecessary c) Wicked

Prurient a) Careful b) Impertinent, overly curious
c) Unhealthily concerned with sex

Recalcitrant a) To be blamed b) Impatient c) Resistant to
authority

Sanitized a) Cleaned up b) Healthy c) Unpleasant smelling

Vainglorious a) Boastful b) Empty-headed c) Vigorous

Verbiage a) Truthfulness b) The use of excessive words
c) Youthfulness

Answers

Acrimonious a) Bitter, full of ill-feeling: *an acrimonious dispute* is rather more than a mild difference of opinion.

Anathema c) Something or someone hateful. Originally a formal excommunication from the Church; now used more loosely, as in *I can't go on crowded trains – they are anathema to me.*

Anodyne a) Dull, bland, as in *an anodyne opinion* or *an anodyne remark*, one that shows no originality and inspires no interest. *Anodyne* also has a medical sense of relieving pain or mental distress and comes from the Greek, meaning painless.

Antipathy a) Dislike – really powerful, strong dislike. The opposite of *sympathy*. See *apathetic*, below.

Apathetic b) Not bothered. The Greek *pathos* means suffering, hence *sympathy* – suffering with someone, sharing their feelings – and *antipathy* (see above), having no fellow feeling. The *a-* at the beginning means not or without, so to be *apathetic* (or to feel *apathy*) is to have no strong feelings on a subject.

Cacophony c) An unpleasant noise. Anything with *phon* in it (*microphone, phonetics, telephone*) is likely to be about sound, and the first part of *cacophony* comes from the Greek for bad. So a *cacophony* is loud, jarring and something you really don't want to listen to. The opposite is *euphony*, a pleasing sound – see *eugenics*, below.

Curmudgeon a) A grumpy person. No one is sure where this word comes from, but it was around at the time of Doctor Johnson's dictionary (1755): he defined it as 'an avaricious churlish fellow; a miser'. Nowadays, the miserliness is less important than the churlishness: you can't be *curmudgeonly* without being bad-tempered.

Dysfunctional a) Abnormal, not functioning. Although it's originally a medical term, it's commonly seen as a description of a family – *a dysfunctional family* being one whose members don't get on and who have an unhealthy effect on each other.

Eugenics b) The study of methods of 'improving' the human race – most often the hideous idea that if you let only the 'right people' have children, you'll end up with a healthier, better species. *Eu-* comes from the Greek for good or pleasant, as in *euphony* (making something, particularly words or combinations of words, sound nice) or *euphemism* (a gentle way of saying something unpleasant, like 'passed away' instead of 'died'). So *eugenics*, whose origins are related to *genes* and *genetics*, is to do with being 'well born'.

Hidebound b) Restricted by petty rules. Imagine a cow whose skin clings to it too tightly because it hasn't been well fed: it is literally *hidebound*. Cautious attitudes or silly regulations can have the same effect on a person or an organization.

Impunity b) A lack of unpleasant consequences. From the same Latin root as *punishment*, doing something *with impunity* means that you get away with it.

Insouciant a) Carefree, often in a slightly unattractive way, not caring about something you *should* care about: *I warned him to drive sensibly, but he gave an insouciant shrug.* From French, so you can, if you like, pronounce the first syllable more like *an* than *in*, and not pronounce the *t* at all.

Intransigent c) Unbending, unwilling to compromise: *an intransigent attitude towards unpunctuality* is one that makes no allowance for traffic or the late running of trains. From Latin words meaning 'not coming to an understanding'.

Magnanimous b) Generous – literally 'great spirited': *it was magnanimous of him not to tell my mother how rude I had been.*

Nefarious c) Wicked, sinful, from the Latin for 'against divine law': *I don't know why he wants to borrow my toolkit, but it's bound to be for some nefarious purpose.*

Prurient c) Unhealthily concerned with sex: *he took a prurient interest in what was going on in the women's changing room*. From the Latin for to itch or to lust after – not nice.

Recalcitrant c) Resistant to authority, stubbornly disobedient: *the recalcitrant kids in her class made the teacher's life a misery*. From Latin meaning to kick out or back.

Sanitized a) Cleaned up, often to excess and often metaphorically: *a sanitized history of a war* might omit all mention of massacres or the bombing of civilians. From the Latin word for health and related to *sanitary* and *sanitation*.

Vainglorious a) Boastful – claiming *glory* in a *vain* or empty way: *those of us who had worked on the senator's campaign knew how lazy he had been; you'd never have guessed it from his vainglorious speech*.

Verbiage b) The use of excessive words, often in a meaningless way: *the first paragraph is all right but the rest is just verbiage – I read the whole article and didn't learn a thing*. Related to *verb* and *verbal*, from the Latin for a word.

CONFUSABLES

metal/mettle

To be *on your mettle* is to be ready to prove yourself; something that *tests your mettle* gives you the opportunity to show yourself at your best. This *mettle* is from an old word meaning courage or strength of character and is nothing to do with the *metals* that include gold, silver and iron.

It's meant as a compliment

But does it mean you're clever, good-natured or good-looking? As ever, it's up to you to decide.

Affable a) Friendly b) Neat and well-groomed c) Plump and cuddly

Altruistic a) Elegant b) Self-confident c) Unselfish

Aplomb a) Cheerfulness b) Elegance c) Self-confidence

Bonhomie a) Elegance b) Friendliness c) Self-confidence

Callipygian a) Having attractive buttocks b) Having long, flowing hair c) Tall and elegant

Dulcet a) Affectionate b) Hard-working c) Sweet-sounding

Ebullient a) Enthusiastic b) Light on one's feet c) Well-educated

Encomium a) Aptitude b) Intelligence c) Praise

Equanimity a) Calmness b) Generosity c) Good looks

Jocular a) Good-humoured b) Merciful c) Plump and cuddly

Kudos a) Acclaim b) An award for loyal service c) Optimism

Mellifluous a) Daintily pretty b) Honey-like c) Wealthy

Munificent a) Generous with money b) Richly dressed c) Splendid

Panegyric a) A formal commendation b) A happy ending
c) A reward for loyal service

Paragon a) A generous donor b) A model of excellence
c) A strikingly handsome man

Pristine a) Beautiful b) Honourable c) Uncorrupted

Pulchritude a) Beauty b) Honesty c) Purity

Redoubtable a) Improbable b) Not able to be put right
c) Worthy of respect

Veracious a) Having a hearty appetite b) Lively c) Truthful

Vivacious a) Dignified b) Open-minded c) Lively

Answers

Affable a) Friendly, good-natured, easy to talk to: *I'd expected the colonel to be rather aloof, but he turned out to be perfectly affable.*

Altruistic c) Unselfish, concerned more for others than for yourself. *An altruistic action* would be performed for the benefit of others, not because you expected credit or money for it.

Aplomb c) Self-confidence, but as a positive attribute, not arrogance. To do something *with aplomb* is to do it not only with confidence but with style. It's an important part of that style not to pronounce the *b*.

Bonhomie b) Friendliness, good-naturedness, from the French *bon homme*, a good man. Though women can have it, too.

Callipygian a) Having attractive buttocks. Yes, there really is a word for that – from the same Greek root as *calligraphy*, meaning beautiful writing. In the Italian National Archaeological Museum in Naples there is a statue known as Aphrodite or Venus Kallipygos; the marble goddess has thoughtfully lifted her robe to one side to reveal her buttocks and whoever named the statue was obviously an admirer.

Dulcet c) Sweet-sounding. This is a word with a perfectly respectable etymology – similar words in French, Italian and Spanish are the standard ones for sweet, soft or gentle – but somehow in English it has become rather ironic. If you spoke of someone's *dulcet tones* or the *dulcet murmur of distant traffic*, the chances are you'd be being sarcastic, while to say something *dulcetly* suggests, to mix a metaphor, that you are hiding an iron fist under that velvet voice.

Ebullient a) Enthusiastic. From the Latin for boiling, so *an ebullient person*, or one in *an ebullient mood*, is bubbling over with excitement.

Encomium c) Praise, particularly in a formal context; the sort of thing that might be said at a retirement party or awards ceremony.

Equanimity a) Calmness, literally 'having an equal mind', not easily upset.

Jocular a) Good-humoured, jokey, from the Latin for a little joke.

Kudos a) Acclaim, prestige: *there's a lot of kudos to be gained from being on the board of the right organization.*

Mellifluous b) Honey-like, particularly of a voice or other sweet sound.

Munificent a) Generous with money, or – of a sum of money – more generous than was necessary or expected: *he donated the munificent sum of £1,000; we'd have been pleased with a couple of hundred.*

Panegyric a) A formal commendation, much the same thing as an *encomium* (see above). The Greek origin of *panegyric* suggests that it is done in public, whereas an *encomium* is part of a festivity, but few people insist on that distinction in modern English.

Paragon b) A model of excellence, someone whose example you would do well to follow – *a paragon of honesty*, for instance, or *a paragon of virtue.*

Pristine c) Uncorrupted, pure, in its original state: if you return an unwanted purchase, the shop will refund your money only if it is *in pristine condition.*

Pulchritude a) Beauty. Not much used in everyday speech – to describe someone as *the embodiment of feminine pulchritude* would sound either pretentious or a bit of a joke.

Redoubtable c) Worthy of respect, formidable, as in *a redoubtable opponent*, one against whom you have to pull out all the stops.

Veracious c) Truthful, from the same Latin root as *veracity*, *verify* and *verisimilitude*, which are all connected with truth.

Vivacious c) Lively, high-spirited, full of *vivacity*. Having a hearty appetite is *voracious*, which is not usually intended as a compliment.

Give them the money

Words about banking, finance and wealth.

Bear market A market in which prices are … a) falling b) rising c) stable

Blue chip A company that is … a) in financial difficulties b) recently launched on the stock market c) regarded as reliable

Capitalization a) A company's total share capital b) Expanding through acquiring another business c) Selling part of a business to raise cash

Collateral a) A company's reputation b) An investment made in the hope of a quick profit c) Security for a loan

Cornucopia a) Abundance b) A company's products viewed as a whole c) Paper money

Disbursement a) A fall in share prices b) Launching a company on the stock market c) A pay-out

Dividend a) A company's annual report b) Dividing a company into several profit centres c) A payment to a shareholder

Emolument a) Bribery b) Profits c) Wages

Equity a) Investments generally b) The net value of a property once debts are paid c) A trust fund

Honorarium a) A payment b) A tribute on retirement c) A well-respected company

Impecunious a) Honourable b) Poor c) Risky

Junk bond a) A fixed-income investment b) An investment with a low return but good long-term prospects c) A holding in a company that has ceased to trade

Largesse a) Generosity with money b) A high profit margin c) A multinational company

Leverage a) Collecting monies due b) The power that comes from being a big company c) 'Selling short', selling stock you don't possess in the hope that prices will fall

Liquidity The ability to ... a) convert assets into money b) ensure a short-term profit c) spread financial risk

Lucrative a) Connected with the oil business b) Dishonest, underhand c) Profitable

Perquisite a) A benefit b) A character reference c) Relevant experience

Portfolio a) A collection of investments b) Documents required for customs purposes c) A report on recent financial activity

Sub-prime a) A child's savings b) A type of mortgage c) An unreliable investment

Tranche a) An instalment, a partial payment b) An interest rate c) A type of investment

Answers

Bear market a) A market in which prices are falling, the opposite of a *bull market*. In the eighteenth century a *bearskin jobber* sold stock he didn't possess, expecting the price to fall so that he could buy cheaply and make a quick profit. Risky, but *lucrative* (see below) if you got it right. The term was soon shortened to *bear*, and the *OED* suggests that it came from the expression *Don't sell the bearskin before you've killed the bear*, meaning much the same as *Don't count your chickens before they're hatched*.

Blue chip c) A company that is regarded as reliable. Blue chips in gambling usually have a high value, so (as the *San Francisco Chronicle* put it in 1847) *if times are good and the market flourishing, the game may be played with 'blue chips', as a gambler would say, the very high-priced stocks being the favourites*.

Capitalization a) A company's total share *capital*, the total number of issued shares multiplied by the share value. The term can be expanded to include money owed to the company and what are known as *retained earnings* – profits that are due to be reinvested back into the business. Anything it possesses or can lay its hands on, in other words.

Collateral c) Security for a loan: *they used their house as collateral to borrow money to expand the business*. From the Latin for *on the side*, because the primary meaning of the word is side by side or parallel – you can have *collateral ridges* in a mountain range, for example, or *a collateral branch of the family*, nephews, nieces and the like rather than direct descendants. *Collateral damage*, that hideous euphemism from modern warfare, comes close to this origin: it's damage (usually deaths of civilians) that occurs alongside the 'legitimate' business of fighting the enemy.

Cornucopia a) Abundance, literally a horn of plenty, often depicted in Classical art as a goat's horn overflowing with corn, fruit and flowers. The god Bacchus may well feature, too (see page 126).

Disbursement c) A pay-out of any kind, often one made on behalf of another: a lawyer or a private investigator might make *disbursements* on behalf of a client (stamp duty, bribes …) and claim these back in addition to their fees. The central part of the word comes from the Latin for a bag or purse and is related to *bursa*, a fluid-containing sac in the body, swelling of which cause *bursitis* or 'housemaid's knee'. Also connected are *La Bourse*, the Paris Stock Exchange, and probably the modern English *purse* as well.

Dividend c) A payment to a shareholder – an allocation from the company's profits paid out to all shareholders in accordance with the number of shares each owns. From the Latin for 'what is to be divided'.

Emolument c) Wages, salary or any other profit arising from employment. A slightly pompous word, given that 'wages' or 'salary' will do perfectly well instead. From the Latin for profit.

Equity b) The net value of a property once debts are paid, usually the share of your house that you, rather than your mortgage lender, actually own. The word comes from the Latin for equal and has other, wider meanings to do with fairness; it's also related to *equilibrium*, *equinox*, *equivalent* and lots of other words connected with equality.

Honorarium a) A payment for a service that is nominally free: *judges at the flower show don't charge a fee, but we give them an honorarium to show our appreciation*. Related to the *honorary degree* for which you haven't actually worked and the *honorary secretary* who doesn't receive a salary; all connected with *honour*.

Impecunious b) Poor, having no money. From the Latin for money. Like *emolument* (above), a fancy word that you should use deliberately, for the fun of it, or not at all.

Junk bond a) A fixed-income investment, yielding a high rate of interest from a company with a low credit rating. Grab the high interest while you can – there's a good chance that the company will default on the payments (or simply go under).

Largesse a) Generosity with money – from the French word meaning broad, which can have the extended idea of being both open-handed and open-minded.

Leverage b) The power that comes from being a big company, being able to use a figurative *lever* to gain an advantage and make things go your way.

Liquidity a) The ability to convert assets into money and pay your debts; having what are called *liquid assets*, rather than everything being tied up in, say, property or stock. *Liquidation* initially meant selling off assets to raise cash; now a company *going into liquidation* tends to be in a desperate situation and the proceeds of the sale don't always cover its losses or satisfy its creditors.

Lucrative c) Profitable, money-making. A perfectly respectable thing for an activity to be, which is odd, given that the noun *lucre* (financial gain or profit, pronounced *luke-er*) from which it comes is rarely used without being qualified by *filthy*.

Perquisite a) A benefit, often shortened to *perk*. This may mean a definite commitment on the part of your employer, such as a company car or free lunches; or it can be used more loosely: *one of the perks of the job was that he could walk to work*. From the Latin, meaning something you have acquired.

Portfolio a) A collection of investments, all the stocks, shares, bonds and what-have-you that an individual or a company possesses; also used with reference to an artist's recent work or a cabinet minister's responsibilities. All these people need something to keep their paperwork together, and *portfolio* (from Italian words meaning 'something to carry papers in') was originally the container rather than the things it contained.

Sub-prime b) A type of mortgage, granted to someone with a credit rating lower than is usually acceptable. Because such a person has a higher risk of defaulting on the payments, lenders often charge higher rates of interest (to cover their own increased risk), setting up a vicious circle that makes it more likely that the borrower is going to default. Someone somewhere not realizing this had a lot to do with the international stock market crash of 2008. The term comes from the concept of a *prime* rate of interest – the rate granted to customers with a decent credit rating.

Tranche a) An instalment, a partial payment of a large sum, as when a company is sold and shareholders receive their money in several stages. A French word, literally a slice.

A fruitful discussion

It's easy to confuse *currant* and *current* but the distinction is clear enough: *currant* is the dried fruit; *current* is everything else. *Current* comes from the Latin for 'to run or flow', so it applies to something that is happening at the moment – *current affairs*, *the current issue of a magazine* – and also to things that flow, such as the *current* in a river or an electrical *current*. *Currency* – the money that is in *current* use – comes from the same source. The name *currant* (the fruit) is a corruption of *Corinth* in Greece, the port from which currants were initially exported to England.

Speaking of dried fruit, a *sultana* is the wife or other female relative of a *sultan*, a title that comes from an Arabic word for to rule. The fruit, which used to be known as a *sultana raisin*, is so named because it originated in parts of the world ruled by a *sultan* – the former Ottoman Empire, centred on modern Turkey.

Wordy words

You can write straightforward sentences with just a subject, a verb and an object: 'You can write a sentence' would be one example. Or you can use various devices to spice up your style. How would you fare on these technical terms?

Alliteration A number of words in quick succession that have the same ... a) initial sound b) number of syllables c) vowel sounds

Antonym A word that ... a) is spelled the same as another word, but pronounced differently b) means the opposite of another c) means the same as another

Apostrophe As well as being a piece of punctuation, is this ... a) addressing an inanimate object b) comparing an inanimate object with a living thing c) talking to oneself?

Apposition a) A deliberate anti-climax for comic effect b) A figure of speech in which a part of something is used to represent the whole c) Placing a word or phrase next to another in order to explain the first

Circumlocution a) An accent used in certain words borrowed from the French b) Direct speech c) A roundabout way of expressing something

Diphthong a) A metrical 'foot' much used by Shakespeare b) Two dots printed over certain vowels c) Two vowels written together and pronounced as one sound

Epigram a) A dedication printed in the opening pages of a book
b) A short final chapter or postscript c) A short, witty remark

Euphemism a) A comparison that states that one thing is like
another b) A novel set in a romantic and idyllic past c) A polite way
of expressing something unpleasant

Hyperbole a) Exaggeration for effect b) A figure of speech in
which a part of something is used to represent the whole c) A word
that is spelled like another, but has a different meaning

Idiom a) An expression used to refer to something indirectly
b) A figure of speech in which an attribute of a thing is used to denote
the thing itself c) A group of words with an established but not literal
meaning

Indicative The form of a verb that … a) expresses doubt b) issues
a command c) makes a statement

Interjection A word that … a) is placed in front of a noun to
show its relationship to the rest of the sentence b) joins two parts of
a sentence c) stands alone grammatically and expresses emotion

Onomatopoeia a) A comparison that suggests one thing is like
another, without actually saying so b) Using two contradictory terms
together c) Using words that reproduce the sound being described

Oxymoron a) A comparison that suggests one thing is like
another, without actually saying so b) Using two contradictory terms
together c) Using words that reproduce the sound being described

Palindrome a) A metrical foot b) A word or group of words that
reads the same backwards as forwards c) Understatement for effect

Paraphrase a) A collective noun b) Comparing an inanimate
object with a living thing c) Expressing something in different words

Personification a) Addressing an inanimate object
b) Attributing human characteristics to non-human things or
qualities c) Comparing two things that are usually considered
opposites

Profanity a) Pompous language b) Something that sounds more
thoughtful than it is c) A swear word

Syntax a) A branch of grammar b) A comparison that suggests one
thing is like another, without actually saying so c) Understatement
for effect

Tautology The use of … a) several adjectives together, to describe
the same noun b) unnecessary words c) words that end in the same
vowel sound but don't rhyme

Trochee a) A deliberate anti-climax b) A metrical foot
c) Understatement for effect

Answers

Alliteration a) A number of words in quick succession that have the same initial sound, as in *grey geese in a green field grazing* or the tongue-twisting *Peter Piper picked a peck of pickled pepper*.

Antonym b) A word that means the opposite of another, such as *good* as opposed to *bad*, *smooth* as opposed to *rough* and so on.

Apostrophe a) Addressing an inanimate object or an imaginary or absent person, breaking off from what you are saying in order to do so. When Macbeth imagines he sees a dagger before him and cries, *Come, let me clutch thee!*, he is *apostrophizing* the dagger.

Apposition c) Placing a word or phrase next to another in order to explain the first, as in *Jack the Giant-Killer* or *Yuri Gagarin, the first man in space*.

Circumlocution c) A roundabout way of expressing something, avoiding getting to the point. *Circum-* means around or surrounding and recurs in *circumference, circumnavigate, circumspect* (literally 'looking around', and by extension 'cautious, considering all the options') and many others. *Locution* comes from the Latin for to speak and can also be found in *elocution* and other words to do with speech. The accent borrowed from French is a *circumflex*, as in *château*.

Diphthong c) Two vowels written together and pronounced as one sound, as in *encyclopædia* and *mediæval*. Also called a *ligature*. Two dots printed over certain vowels are a *diaeresis* – this shows that the vowel in question is pronounced separately, as in *naïve*, which doesn't rhyme with *waive*.

Epigram c) A short, witty remark. A dedication printed in the opening pages of a book is an *epigraph*; a short final chapter is an *epilogue*.

Euphemism c) A polite way of expressing something unpleasant, as in *passed away* for *dying*, or various means of discussing sex or bodily functions in words of more than four letters. See also *eugenics*, page 159.

Hyperbole a) Exaggeration for effect, as in *I've told you a million times*, when the truth is you've probably mentioned it on three or four occasions.

Idiom c) A group of words with an established but not literal meaning. One of the defining features of an idiom is that you *can't* deduce its meaning from the words it contains: *letting the cat out of the bag* has nothing to do with cats or bags, while if you took *barking up the wrong tree* literally, you would assume you had to be a dog to do it. An expression used to refer to something indirectly is an *allusion*; a figure of speech in which an attribute of a thing is used to denote the thing itself – such as 'Washington' for 'American politics' – is a *metonymy*.

Indicative c) The form of a verb that makes a statement or asks a question, such as *makes* and *asks* in this sentence. Expressing doubt is done with the *subjunctive* (see page 96) and commands are issued with the *imperative*: *Do this! Don't do that!*

Interjection c) A word that stands alone grammatically and expresses emotion – *Aha! Alas!* or just *Oh!* A word in front of a noun showing its relationship to the rest of the sentence (*at*, *on*, *to* and a host of short words along those lines) is a *preposition*; two parts of a sentence are joined by a *conjunction*.

Onomatopoeia c) Using words that reproduce the sound being described, such as *buzz*, *fizz* or *quack*; or putting a number of words together to produce that effect, as in Tennyson's *the murmuring of innumerable bees*. See the box on page 177.

Oxymoron b) Using two contradictory terms together, as in *bitter sweet* or, as Juliet put it when she was taking her time saying goodnight to Romeo, *parting is such sweet sorrow*.

Palindrome b) A word or group of words that reads the same backwards as forwards – *civic*, *kayak*, *Madam, I'm Adam* or *A man, a plan, a canal, Panama*. Don't worry about any punctuation or spaces between the words: as long as the letters themselves fit the pattern, it's a palindrome.

Paraphrase c) Expressing something in different words, often to make the idea clearer. A clause in a will may contain the words *all my real and personal estate not hereby or by any codicil hereto otherwise* *specifically disposed of*; this could be *paraphrased* as *everything I possess* or *all my stuff*.

Personification b) Attributing human characteristics to non-human things or qualities: *the sun smiled on us on the day of the picnic*. It didn't, of course – the sun is a huge sphere of hot gas. It doesn't smile. But hey. You know what I mean.

Profanity c) A swear word or other coarse or disrespectful language. From the Latin for 'outside the temple', *profane* originally meant not initiated into sacred rites, not admitted into the inner sanctum; from that it developed into blaspheming, showing irreverence for something sacred, and then into more general forms of abusive language and discourtesy.

Syntax a) A branch of grammar, concerned with the way words fit together in a sentence, as opposed to the form of the words themselves. What we often describe as poor grammar – as in the misrelated participle *Hanging out the clothes, the blackbird pecked off her nose* – is actually poor syntax. (In case you're wondering, that example says that the blackbird was hanging out the clothes, which isn't the most likely scenario.)

Tautology b) The use of unnecessary words, repeating a meaning that has already been expressed: *an unconfirmed rumour*, for instance, or *a free gift*. The point here is that once something has been confirmed, it ceases to be a rumour; if it isn't free, it isn't a gift.

Trochee b) A metrical foot consisting of a long syllable followed by a short one, as in the line from Edgar Allen Poe's poem 'The Raven': *Quoth the Raven 'Nevermore'*. Understatement for effect, the opposite of *hyperbole* (see above) is *litotes*: *He seemed quite pleased to have won the lottery*.

I like the sound of that

Poets, in particular, love *onomatopoeia* (see page 175), but it can be expressive for the rest of us, too. We have words that sound like:

- running water – *babble, burble, gurgle*
- bells ringing – *ding, dong, jingle, jangle*
- the noises animals make – *baa, meow, moo, oink, quack, woof*
- explosions – *bang, boom, pop* – or speeding bullets – *zip, zoom*
- things we have just trodden on – *crunch, rustle, squelch* – or set fire to – *crackle, sizzle* – or dropped – *clunk, crash, smash*

We *cackle* and *hiccup*, our stomachs *rumble*. The wind *whooshes* past us or *whispers* or *murmurs* in the trees. Drinks *fizz*, doorbells *buzz*, fridges *hum* – it's a wonder we can hear ourselves think.

Words that are a joy to use

~

English is full of these – words that are so expressive that you want to work them into your conversation whenever you can. If they are words of anger or disapproval, you can almost spit them out; if they're affectionate, you feel you are stroking them. These are just twenty that I happen to like and that haven't found a place anywhere else in the book.

Abomination a) An explosion b) A hateful, disgusting thing
c) An unpleasant smell

Behemoth a) An earnest request b) An enormous beast
c) A swear word

Callow a) Discreet b) Inexperienced c) Pale, unhealthy looking

Extirpate a) To annoy b) To get rid of c) To pardon

Frenetic a) Absent-minded b) Agitated c) Threatening

Garrulous a) Careless b) Hostile c) Talkative

Grandiloquent a) Generous b) Having many talents c) Pompous

Gratuitous a) Grateful b) Hurried c) Unnecessary

Hapless a) Accidental b) Infrequent c) Unfortunate

Hirsute a) Chaotic b) Hairy c) Shiny

Hoodwink a) To deceive b) To invent c) To persist

Inchoate a) At an early stage b) Impolite c) Uncomfortable

Lothario a) A layabout b) A miser c) A womanizer

Miscreant a) A mischievous child b) A mistake, inaccuracy
c) A villain

Platitude a) A boring remark b) A disappointment c) A nest-egg,
savings

Pugnacious a) Exhausting b) Lively c) Ready for a fight

Quagmire a) An awkward situation b) Financial difficulty
c) A tedious job

Quintessential a) Basic, lacking in luxury b) Speedy c) Typical

Ubiquitous a) Disciplined b) Found everywhere c) Quick-witted

Umbrage a) Approval b) A fair share c) Offence

Answers

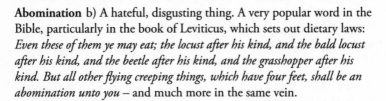

Abomination b) A hateful, disgusting thing. A very popular word in the Bible, particularly in the book of Leviticus, which sets out dietary laws: *Even these of them ye may eat; the locust after his kind, and the bald locust after his kind, and the beetle after his kind, and the grasshopper after his kind. But all other flying creeping things, which have four feet, shall be an abomination unto you* – and much more in the same vein.

Behemoth b) Another biblical word, this is an enormous beast that appears in the book of Job, mentioned in the same passage as a sea monster called the *leviathan*. Both words have come to mean anything that is huge and difficult to control.

Callow b) Inexperienced, naïve about life, often in the expression *a callow youth*. From a Germanic word meaning bald, which led to 'unfledged, not yet fully feathered', as a description of an immature bird, and then to a less clearly defined form of immaturity in young people.

Extirpate b) To get rid of completely. Literally, to clear out the stump of a tree, but more often used figuratively: *the government promised to extirpate all traces of corruption.*

Frenetic b) Agitated, frenzied, moving at a fast and frantic pace: *the kitchen was a scene of frenetic activity – sandwiches were being made, scones baked and cakes iced, all at the same time.* Related to *frantic* and deriving from words for delirium and mental illness.

Garrulous c) Talkative to a fault and unlikely to say much worth listening to, from a Latin word for to chatter: *I had to shut myself in my bedroom to get away from my garrulous aunts and stop them telling me stories I had heard many times before.*

Grandiloquent c) Pompous, literally 'large speaking': *the mayor spoke in a grandiloquent manner that showed he expected us to agree with everything he said.*

Gratuitous c) Unnecessary, uncalled for. From the Latin meaning free of charge, this originally meant 'freely bestowed, given without expecting payment'. Over the years it acquired negative connotations, so that we now have *gratuitous violence* in films and on television and *gratuitous insults* when someone feels like being rude to us.

Hapless c) Unfortunate, a victim of circumstances beyond your control. *Hap* is an old word for luck or chance, related to *happen* and *happy*. To be *hapless*, therefore, is to lack *hap*: *the hapless newcomer was no match for his more experienced and more cunning colleagues*. See also *feckless*, page 153, and the box on page 155.

Hirsute b) Hairy, in an unkempt sort of way, from the Latin for bristly. You might apply it jokingly to someone who has just grown a beard, or disapprovingly to someone who has let his beard get out of control.

Hoodwink a) To deceive. Originally to put a hood over someone's head to blindfold them; now, metaphorically, to pull the wool over their eyes, to trick them: *he hoodwinked me into going to the dance by promising me great music, but it turned out to be one man and a banjo.*

Inchoate a) At an early stage, undeveloped. From a Latin word meaning to begin, this often refers to ideas or policies that are in their infancy: *she struggled to assemble her inchoate thoughts – she hadn't had time to think the matter through*. Pronounced *in-ko-ate*.

Lothario c) A womanizer, a libertine. From a character in a seventeenth-century story by Miguel de Cervantes and another in a later play, *The Fair Penitent* by Nicholas Rowe. In both cases, Lothario seduces the main female character; in the latter, he betrays her and allows posterity to give him a bad name.

Miscreant c) A villain – originally an unbeliever or heretic (from the Latin for to believe wrongly), but now a more broadly based wrongdoer: *the police caught the miscreant trying to sell the stolen jewellery.*

Platitude a) A boring remark, a commonplace observation that has been heard many times before: *she talked entirely in platitudes, never discussing anything but the weather and the Royal Family and not saying anything interesting about them*. From the French for flat.

Pugnacious c) Ready for a fight, aggressive in attitude and manner. Useful for describing the sort of person who would ask, 'Are you looking at me?' and offer to meet you outside. From the Latin for fight.

Quagmire a) An awkward situation. Literally, a marsh that sinks under your feet (a *quaggy mire*); metaphorically, a set of circumstances in which you get bogged down: *once news of the scandal had broken, he had to wade through a quagmire of embarrassing questions.*

Quintessential c) Typical – the most typical representation of something. As in *he was the quintessential Englishman, bowler hat, rolled umbrella and all.* From the Latin for 'fifth essence', because in medieval philosophy ether or *quintessence* was the fifth element (after air, fire, water and earth), believed to be the essential ingredient of the heavenly bodies.

Ubiquitous b) Found everywhere; from the Latin for everywhere. This has theological uses, referring to the omnipresence of God, but is also used to describe someone or something that *seems* to be everywhere: *a ubiquitous actor* has appeared in umpteen films and television series lately, while *the ubiquitous pomegranate juice* seems to feature on every trendy health-food menu.

Umbrage c) Offence, especially in the expression *to take umbrage*: *he took umbrage at her behaviour and never invited her again.* From a French word for shade or shadow, which went through various subtle shifts in meaning to give the modern sense.

Words that are a joy to use (2)

Twenty words were far too few for this category, so – just for the joy of including them – here are twenty more.

Apotheosis a) Disgust b) Glorification c) Preparation, recipe

Babel a) Confusion b) Criticism c) Sulking

Cantankerous a) Bad-tempered b) Drunken c) Muddy

Carapace a) A competition b) A protective covering c) A silky material

Consummate a) Deceptive b) Greedy c) Highly skilled

Diaphanous a) Fine, delicate b) Isolated c) Untrustworthy

Festoon a) To decorate b) To hurry c) To spend extravagantly

Gamut a) Annoyance b) Destruction c) Range

Ignominy a) Disgrace b) Stupidity c) Worthlessness

Importunate a) Demanding b) Necessary c) Unlucky

Neophyte a) A chemical b) A forgetful person c) A new convert, a beginner

Oleaginous a) Drowsy b) Oily c) Unpleasantly scented

Parlous a) Dangerous b) Equal c) Talkative

Philistine A person who … a) is bad-tempered b) doesn't care about the arts and culture c) doesn't known their own strength

Presentiment a) A presentation b) A sense of something bad to come c) A summons to appear in court

Proclivity a) Fertility b) An inclination c) A rapid movement

Quotidian a) Everyday b) Extravagantly literary c) Newsworthy

Soporific a) Painful b) Sleep-inducing c) Thought-provoking

Spasmodic a) Occurring in brief spurts b) Shining, sparkling c) Strict

Unwitting a) Reluctant b) Stupid c) Unaware

CONFUSABLES

discreet/discrete

Discreet means tactful, not likely to give away a secret; *discrete* is separate: *he kept the specimens in discrete compartments so that they wouldn't contaminate each other, but he asked me to be discreet about his experiments.*

Answers

∿

Apotheosis b) Glorification, literally making someone or something into a god (the *theo* in the middle of the word is from the Greek for god, which also gives us *theology* – see *pantheism*, page 25). The meaning of *apotheosis* can drift away from godliness, though, and become something more like the highest point of excellence: *Italian sculpture reached its apotheosis with the work of Michelangelo.*

Babel a) Confusion, from the biblical story of the Tower of Babel. At one time, all the people on Earth spoke one language and they agreed to build a tower that would reach Heaven. God, not convinced that this was a good idea, 'confounded their language', so that they couldn't understand each other and couldn't work together. He also scattered them across the Earth, so that they left their great tower unfinished. The city it was in was called Babel, and the word has come to mean any noisy and confused discussion: *a babel of voices* is one in which there is a lot of talking but you can't make sense of it.

Cantankerous a) Bad-tempered, always ready to pick a quarrel. Often applied to an elderly person (*a cantankerous old so-so*) who takes a certain grim satisfaction from telling you that the world is going to the dogs. Probably from a Middle English word for quarrel.

Carapace b) A protective covering, specifically the hard shell of creatures such as tortoises and crabs. Also used metaphorically: *antidepressants seemed like a carapace that protected me from problems I found hard to cope with.*

Consummate c) Highly skilled. *Consummation* is about completion, so to *consummate* a marriage is to complete it (by having sex). Used as an adjective, therefore, *consummate* means 'complete, having reached a pinnacle of achievement': *a consummate pianist*, perhaps, or *a consummate liar.*

∿

Diaphanous a) Fine, delicate and semi-transparent, used of a light fabric such as silk: *she wore a diaphanous veil that protected her complexion without causing her to bump into people in the street.* From the Greek for transparent.

Festoon a) To decorate lavishly. A *festoon* (from an Italian word related to *feast*) is a garland of flowers, ribbons or the like, hung in loops like Christmas decorations. The meaning can be extended to embrace other forms of adornment, as long as they are extravagant: *she was festooned with diamonds and furs.*

Gamut c) Range, the full extent over which something – usually emotions – can spread. Often in the expression *to run the gamut*: *he ran the gamut from pathos to fury,* or, in the memorable insult attributed to the American wit Dorothy Parker, *she ran the whole gamut of emotions from A to B. Gamut* is originally a musical term, abbreviated from the names of two notes, *gamma* and *ut,* and meaning the range of notes generally recognized in medieval music, or, later, the range an individual instrument can cover.

Ignominy a) Disgrace, particularly public disgrace. This and its adjective *ignominious* convey real disgust: *his career ended in ignominy when it was revealed he had been embezzling for years* or *it was an ignominious attempt to deceive the voting public.* The central part of these words comes from the Latin *nomen,* 'name', so loss of reputation or good name is an important part of their meaning.

Importunate a) Demanding, asking persistently and annoyingly for something: *if he'd asked sensibly I'd have let him drive my car, but he was so importunate that I got cross and refused.* From a Latin word for tiresome and inconvenient – it's part of the subtext of *importuning* someone that, not only are you being a pest, but you have picked the wrong moment.

Neophyte c) A new convert, a beginner, with overtones of both enthusiasm and naïveté. Lots of words beginning with *neo-* are to do with newness (*neologism,* a newly coined word; *Neolithic,* belonging to the newest or most recent part of the Stone Age). A *neophyte* is literally 'newly planted' in a religious faith, but the word can also be applied in a wider context: *the gymkhana was designed to appeal equally to neophytes and to experienced riders.*

Oleaginous b) Oily, from the Latin *olea*, an olive tree. Although the word can be used to describe the products of the olive, it's more likely to be found with reference to a person – a bit creepy and overly eager to please: *he had a limp, sweaty handshake, an oleaginous manner and a voice that managed to sound flattering and sinister at the same time.* A description to be applied to someone you really don't like.

Parlous a) Dangerous, on the brink of disaster – related to *perilous*: *an expensive holiday was out of the question with my finances in such a parlous state.*

Philistine b) A person who doesn't care about the arts and culture. In the Old Testament of the Bible, the Philistine tribe was constantly at war with the Israelites; the giant Goliath, slain by David, was one of them. The attributes now associated with their name are not only ignorance of culture but a positive reluctance to learn anything about it; unsophisticated tastes and a general lack of appreciation of the finer things of life: *there's no point in taking him to a smart restaurant; he's a philistine and would rather have a burger.*

Presentiment b) A sense of something bad to come. *Presentment* (without the *i*) has various meanings connected with formal *presentations* in the Church or in a court of law. Add the *i*, however, and you have a *pre-sentiment*, with *pre-* meaning 'before'; thus, *a sentiment* felt in advance. It doesn't absolutely have to be bad, but it generally is, often *a presentiment of disaster* or *a presentiment of impending doom.*

Proclivity b) An inclination, usually towards something not quite proper. It's from the Latin for a slope and the implication is that the slope is both downward and slippery: *his proclivity for lying to save his own skin will get him into trouble one of these days.*

Quotidian a) Everyday, possibly literally, in the simple sense of 'occurring every day', but more often 'boring, nothing out of the ordinary': *the quotidian view of row upon row of dull grey houses made her long for the delights of Florence or Venice.*

Soporific b) Sleep-inducing, either literally or figuratively: *Peter Rabbit succumbed to the soporific properties of lettuce* or *it was the most soporific lecture I had ever been to – I only hope I didn't snore.*

Spasmodic a) Occurring in brief spurts or *spasms*, a spasm being a muscular contraction that causes cramp-like pain. In the figurative sense, you can have *spasmodic bursts of activity* in the middle of an otherwise lazy day, or *spasmodic fits of temper* if things aren't going your way.

Unwitting c) Unaware, not knowing, as in *he was the unwitting cause of the row – he hadn't realized he would upset anyone*. From an old word *wit*, meaning to know and loosely connected with the modern sense of *wit*: 'clever, humorous speech or writing'. The earlier meaning is preserved in the phrase *to wit*, 'that is to say': *I make the same New Year's resolution every year – to wit, no alcohol in January.*

Index